Outside Disneyland

by Jay Kesler & Tim Stafford

Outside Disneyland

Practical Christianity for Real-Life Hassles

Word Books, Publisher

Waco, Texas

Outside Disneyland

The Scripture quotation marked Phillips is from **The New Testament in Modern English,** copyright ⓒ 1958, 1959, 1960, 1972 by J. B. Phillips; used by permission of The MacMillan Company. All other quotations are from **The Living Bible, Paraphrased** (Wheaton: Tyndale House Publishers, 1971) and are used by permission.

Printed in the United States of America. Library of Congress catalog card number: 77–075465

Contents

how can I stop feeling lonely?

Loneliness is the most normal thing in the world. Doesn't everyone feel like getting off alone and figuring things in his own head?

Not long ago I met a girl with very deep problems. Joan was considering suicide.

She told me it began with feeling lonely. She was going through a lot of things, as are most people in high school, and sometimes she felt like no one understood her or liked her. She tended to stay around the house, and she often acted moody. Her mother couldn't understand that. She said, "There must be something wrong with you." Then she started telling Joan she ought to see a counselor. That may not have been a bad idea, but to Joan only sick people saw counselors. So it reinforced the idea that because she felt lonely, she was sick. And that idea got stronger and stronger, until she was ready to go off the deep end.

I talked to Joan for a long time and stressed one fact again and again—everybody is lonely. It's the most normal thing in the world. Nearly all humans feel rejected and lonely at times, even in crowds, and nearly all humans want to go off alone sometimes and work things out in their own heads.

That simple fact, plus some other hints on how to deal with lonely feelings, really helped Joan. I got a letter from her not long afterwards, and she sounded like a different person. She'd done a complete turnaround, because she'd accepted the fact that it wasn't necessarily weird to feel lonely.

That's the kind of problem loneliness is—it feeds on itself. Lonely feelings make you burrow into yourself, make you look at the rest of the world as though it's very different from you. And that makes your loneliness worse. If you can relax and accept loneliness as normal, you're in position to do something helpful with it.

Most of the lonely people I've talked to are afraid. They're sure other people won't accept them. They have a set of assumptions about what other people think of them; they tend to say, "I know what they're thinking." Consequently, they isolate themselves.

But the assumptions are usually way off. Most of those other people aren't self-assured either. Most of them aren't out to look down on people. The truth is, most of "them" are as lonely and miserable as you are. Even the people who make a habit of putting you down—they're not doing that because they hate you. They do it because they've got problems of their own, and you happen to be in the way when they look for someone to snub. They're really using put-downs and fake self-confidence as defense mechanisms to hide their own loneliness.

I don't say that's always true, and I don't say it's easy to penetrate those defense mechanisms. But I do believe that if you take your assumptions about other people out and look at them, you'll find they're not based on much evidence. How do you know what they think of you? Look at your feelings, and then start assuming other people feel exactly the same way. You want a friend? Okay, assume they want a friend, and you'll be right 90 percent of the time. You like most people? So does 90 percent of the world, which means they very probably like you. Try going through a day at school just assuming that everyone you know basically likes and admires you.

Chances are very good the evidence in favor of that assumption will pile up. So what if someone doesn't respond to that assumption? He's only among the 10 percent.

But how do you find the courage and self-confidence to act on your new assumptions?

There's a famous story about a man who tried to peel an onion. He kept taking off layer after layer, looking for the real onion inside. Only after he'd taken off everything did he realize that an onion is all peel. There is no core, no real fruit inside.

Many times I feel like that's a symbol of my life. I'm all peel; when you've stripped away all my attitudes and relationships, there's nothing left. And then it's very simple to feel lonely, and it's very hard to be outgoing. If I'm rejected, what have I got left over? There's no core.

That's one of the primary reasons I'm a Christian. Christ is the core of my life, and one solid thing that exists in my world. He will never leave me or forsake me. He will stay with me no matter what I am. He accepts me unconditionally.

With that as a basis, my human relationships become a kind of bonus. I'm not risking everything when I meet someone. A lot of kids never risk themselves in relationships because, subconsciously, they feel that if things go wrong they've lost everything. A Christian doesn't have to feel that way, because Christ is always a friend who sticks closer than a brother.

And Jesus knows how you feel. You know, he took the first and biggest risk of rejection. He came into our world without any armor to protect him. He came as a normal human being, without any flashing signs that said, "I'm God." He came and experienced total rejection. He wants to be with you when you take the same kind of risks while reaching out to other people. You can always fall back on him.

I need friends

Last week I had a guy come up to me and say, "I've never had a date. I don't feel I've ever had a friend. I've always felt like everyone was too busy for me. I always stand at the edge of conversations, and people never include me. I feel completely alone, completely rejected, and I don't know how to handle it."

So we talked about his problems. He knew Christ, and said he felt close to him. But he said, "That's not enough. I need more in life. I need people to like me."

And I had to agree with him. God didn't create us to be hermits. He made us with personality, with the capacity for friendship and loyalty. He made us so we'd be lonely when we didn't have friends, so that we would go out and find some.

I asked him, "Can you think of anyone else who might feel lonely, too? Some girl who is too shy to have friends? Some guy who feels like he's never accomplished much? If so, do you think it's possible you have something to offer them? It might help you to take your mind off your own problems and put it on other people's."

We were at a camp. During the rest of the time I was there I watched him trying the experiment. He'd walk up to kids who were sitting on the grass by themselves, or who were on the outskirts of a crowd, and he'd talk to them. And, naturally, they were glad to talk to him.

You want to be accepted? Work at accepting people. You feel people reject you? Work at not giving other people rejection signs every time they try to find a way into your friendship. I'm talking about the Golden Rule here—do unto others as you want them to do to you. That's not just a trite, moralistic phrase. It's a practical way of going about life. It works. People who practice it tend to have fewer troubles relating to other people, and they end up happier.

There's one thing you must avoid—coming on hard and doing a lot of talking. Show-offs do that, and they're usually showing that they're the most insecure and needy people of all. They sometimes do get attention, but they rarely get understanding and love, which is what they really need.

One of the rules of life is that people are interested in themselves. When you start applying the Golden Rule as a way of opening your life to friendship, you start by listening a lot. You ask questions. You try to find whether there is some area of another person's life he wants to talk about—not just problems, but areas where he really has some confidence. Listening is one of the basic rules of conversation, but it's something that a lot of lonely kids don't understand. They only want to talk, and pretty soon the person who's listening gets tired of it.

It's an unrealistic goal to expect to be popular with everyone overnight, and I doubt it's all that desirable. Having a lot of not-so-close friends is nice, but they may not keep you from feeling lonely. What's much more important is to have one or two very close friends with whom you can be completely honest. And that's a rare thing—it's a very happy man or woman who has even one.

But again, in trying to find that close friendship, most lonely people make the wrong assumptions. They don't understand that friendship is based on sharing weakness, not strength. They go and try to impress people with how neat they are, and are surprised when that doesn't work. They think the football hero and the basketball hero have friends just because they're strong. But those people, if their popularity is genuine, probably make friends the same way everyone else does—by sharing weakness.

It's not the kind of sharing you do all the time, or that you do with someone you just met. You do it very gingerly and very tenderly. You have to be sensitive to the right time, and you have to leave it open for the other person to share something with you if he wants to.

Of course, very lonely people often want to go out and become close friends with the most popular and vivacious people. It seldom happens. For one thing, the sharing would be unequal. If you're shy and insecure, it's very difficult to get the courage to share even a small personal fear or weakness. It may seem like nothing at all to the self-confident kid who's so secure he can talk about his complexion or about sex without batting an eye. Sharing, if it's to build deep friendship, should be something equal. You have to start with people more or less like yourself.

Maybe you say, "I don't want to be friends with other lonely kids; I want the popular kids for my friends." That tells me something about where your values are, and I'll say more about that later. But as a practical matter, remember that no baseball player starts in the majors. You start down in the minors. The minors aren't a put-down; they provide a place where you're on a peer level and can really develop. When your skills have developed you aren't overwhelmed by better players anymore, and you can fit easily into another league and continue to grow.

Friendships can be the same. If you try to hang around a gang that's much more free and secure than you are personally, you'll never grow. You'll just end up as a loose end, or you might turn into a show-off just to get attention. Start with people on your level of loneliness and insecurity. Learn some of the rules of friendship with them, and you may develop enough security to expand your horizons. That doesn't mean, of course, that you drop the "lower" group for a group with more status: it just means that you've become comfortable with a wider group of people.

One other thing I've seen kids do effectively is build their own self-confidence by finding an area they can succeed in. This tends to sound corny, and it can be overstressed. But it can really help, too.

Not long ago I was on a version of a Mississippi paddleboat, taking a tour of a lake in Wisconsin. I saw a guy there who appeared lonely. He was standing off to the side a little, and I felt sorry for him.

I stood by the edge of the boat near him, and started looking down at the paddle wheels turning in the water. I didn't say anything. After a while I spit in the water, and then he spit into it. Then I said to him, "This is really a nice paddle boat, isn't it?" And he said, "This isn't a paddle boat." I said, "It isn't?" He said, "Oh, no, this is just a reproduction. That paddle doesn't really do anything. This thing is run by a propeller. This is just kind of a tourist thing.

"Now the real thing," he said, "works this way . . ." And for about an hour I got an extremely interesting lecture on Mississippi paddle boats. This guy had really become an expert, and he could talk about it in an interesting manner.

There are two lessons you can learn from that. First, when you reach out to someone, it helps if you can locate their area of confidence and let them express themselves in it. If I'd tried to stir up a conversation with that guy about all the girls I'd dated, it probably wouldn't have gotten too far.

Second, you can learn that an area where you're confident is a valuable thing. Suppose a guy feels lonely because his school puts tremendous emphasis on athletics, and he can't play basketball. Well, there are a lot of ways he could go. He could become a sports writer for the school paper, and find an in on sports that way. Another kid might go off and become a good musician. Instead of finding friends in athletics, he could find friends in the band, or among other musicians. My own son right now is interested in canaries. That may sound like a weird thing, but it's an interest area for him. He goes to pet shops, and finds people who really think it's something to know about canaries. He has a place.

Unfortunately, many kids are not happy with the interest group they can cultivate. They may be good stamp collectors but they want to be good fullbacks. Well, if they spend all their time feeling that way, they'll end up lonely. In fact, there's something kind of sad about a guy who has to constantly hang around the locker room when he's never made it as an athlete. He's telegraphing his lack of self-confidence by pretending to be something he's not. You've got to learn to live with the abilities you've got, and forget the ones you don't have.

Personally, I realized long ago that I wasn't going to be a great athlete. I tried, you know. I played basketball a lot, but when I got to be a freshman in high school I couldn't make the team. So I became a manager. I found out it didn't have to be a demeaning experience. Sure, certain insecure guys may make fun of the manager, but that's no big

deal. It gave me a place that had value and built my
friendship with a lot of guys.

the ugly and unlovely

Okay, you say, so I follow your advice. I end up
with a bunch of friends who are ugly, incapable, and
unlovely. I spend time with other lonely people. I'm
in a group all right, but it's a group that nobody
cares about.

There's something wrong with that whole line of
thinking. It ranks people in status according to how
athletic they are, or how good-looking. But as I
understand it, young people say again and again
that you can't judge a person by how he looks, that
people who don't achieve the "important" things
aren't worthless, that everybody's different and has
to find his own way. Kids say, "It isn't important
what you look like, it's what you are."

But do you really believe that? Probably not.
When you go looking for friends you want one of
the really well-liked, well-thought-of people to notice
you. It really comes down to status, just like it did
to the older generation who judged someone by his
clothes or how much money he made.

Personally, I've found those values worthless in
the long haul. A lot of the people who seem to have
nothing to offer turn out to be my most treasured
friends. And the people who have all the status often
turn out to be nothing. Why? A lot of times it's because they got status through their genes. The girl
had a pretty face, or the guy had a great body, or
they were born into the right families. That made

them liked. But when the bodies had gone downhill, what was left? They'd never developed the kind of inner strength that went beyond those things.

To develop real strength as a person, start where you are. If you're talented in something, develop that. Start with people you can relate to as a peer. Try treating everybody the way you want them to treat you. And learn to expect that 90 percent of the world is as lonely and hungry for friendship as you are.

If you do that, you're going to find, sooner or later, that you're rarely lonely. You find you can enter different groups and feel at ease. You have one or two intimate friends with whom you can share anything about yourself. Your relationship with Jesus is deep and strong, so that you can risk rejection from people because you're sure of his support.

Then what do you do?

You begin to reach out to include other people.

They once used a word to describe people who were really at the top—**exclusive.** It's not a current word, but it still describes the way a lot of the most popular people function; they stay at the top by excluding others. Carl Sandburg said once that **exclusive** is the ugliest word in the English language. I think I agree. I think the Bible would agree.

The Christian responsibility is this: whenever you're with a group that's forming a little circle, and you see someone standing out on the edge, step back a couple of steps and invite the other person into the circle. No Christian should ever allow people to stand outside the circle. You've got to break the circle, physically and symbolically. Step back and say, "Join us." If you're going somewhere, say, "Why don't you come along?" Pretty soon you find a spirit developing in yourself and even in your group. You're inclusive instead of exclusive. If more Christians were like that, there would be fewer lonely people.

is death the end?

This marvelous body of mine . . . these feelings inside . . . will death evaporate them and leave only darkness?

You are in a dark place. Warm. Comfortable. Secure. Your eyes are closed and you rock gently back and forth. There is no pain, no noise but the rhythmic beating of your own heart.

Suddenly you feel motion. Something is pulling at your head, pressing down all around you. You feel pressure. You're stretched. Your feet are twisted against your body at a warped angle. You're sucked through a narrow tunnel of pulsating pressure and suddenly emerge in a room of loud noises and blinding lights. It's strange, painful, scary, and you begin to cry.

You have just experienced birth.

Would you really want to go back to the womb? Yes, birth meant pain, fright, and loneliness, and the life you entered was full of problems. But would you really go back if offered the chance?

Joe Bayly, a Christian author, says the experience of death must be very much like birth. It can be scarier, since we're more sophisticated and aware when we face death. But the process is about the same—a little darkness, a little pain, then a whole new world outside.

You may be comfortable now, but sooner or later you, too, will be squeezed through the long tunnel of death into a new world. What's out there? Is there any way we can know for sure?

don't let her suffer

I have watched quite a few different people die. Some of them were close to me, and some I'd never seen before. Some died quietly in hospital beds, and some bled out their lives beside a highway. Every time I see someone die, it changes me a little, I think.

I remember one experience particularly well. I was in Southern California, on a freeway crowded with people going to the Rose Bowl. A new year was starting.

Then I saw the accident. A car carrying a load of kids had turned over and the car was upside down, the wheels still spinning. I pulled over and went from person to person, seeing if I could do anything to help. There was one girl who had virtually nothing left of her face. She was crying, in terrible pain. I held her in my arms; there was nothing else I could do. I found myself praying, "God, take her now . . ." And he did take her; she died right there while I watched her.

Thinking back over that experience still makes me feel frightened. But why? Why was it such a strong experience for me? I knew then and I know now that people die on the highways every day. I hear the reports on the radio, and it doesn't affect me at all. I certainly didn't know that particular girl; she hadn't meant anything to me. The only difference between her death and the thousands I hear about every year was that I happened to be there when it happened. Yet it moved me in a way few things in life do.

The reason that's so is that it made the reality of my own death much more real. It could have been me; my car could have been the one flipped upside down, and I could have been the person crying and trying to gasp a few last breaths. Of course, I'd known that all along. I know there's a reason I have to buy car insurance just like everyone else. I'm not Superman, and statistically I'm as likely to die as the next person. But that girl, whose name I don't even know, brought death out of the realm of statistics and obituary pages, and into bone and blood. For quite a while after that experience I couldn't ignore the fact that I, Jay Kesler, was going to die. It was a frightening realization.

putting death in a closet

The fear of death is coming out into the open these days, at least with young people. I think that's good, basically. For a long time people have tried to put death in a closet and lock the door. You can ignore death in our society; people don't die in the home very often, as they once did. Old people live in nursing homes, and kids never see them when they're sick and dying.

But despite that people are, if anything, more afraid of death than ever before. If you offer seminars at a camp, where kids are free to choose which one to attend, death will usually outdraw any other topic. That includes sex. There is a wave of newly published books on death. TV shows deal specifically with death.

It's not just idle curiosity feeding the interest. It's fear. Some are more afraid than others, of course, but nearly all of us are in some way afraid of death. Elisabeth Kübler-Ross, the international expert on death, says the fear of death is like something big, horrible and horrendous that is bearing down on you. It's dark, unknown, unstoppable. Death gives you a feeling of complete helplessness.

Ratso shuffles off

Why is death so frightening? One reason is, I suspect, that we're not sure how we will die. Will our lives end on an heroic note, or will we go out with a whimper? We know we should live in a manner that leaves us ready to die—but how? One movie that seems to have symbolized the hopelessness of life and death to many people is **Midnight Cowboy,** shown recently on TV. The story is about two drifters who meet in New York City. They're a likable pair, and they go through a number of interesting adventures just trying to survive. But in the end Ratso dies, coughing his life out in the back of a Greyhound bus going to Florida. The audience has been rooting for him, and then he just shuffles into death, useless and purposeless, just as he lived.

People I know came away from **Midnight Cowboy** telling me no movie had depressed them so much. They'd seen themselves in Ratso, funny and interesting and wily, and then the movie had played a trick on them and they'd seen themselves as the same Ratso who died a pathetic, pointless death. Nothing about Ratso, however funny or interesting he was, was really worth much when you added it all up.

So we wonder, will my life end like that? Will anyone remember me? Will I just shuffle off the stage, telling jokes and trying to act as though I know what I'm doing? Because so many of the things I spend my energy on are just like Ratso. I want to be admired, I want to be funny, I want to be handsome, I want to be capable. But how much of what I do in life is worth dying for? Or living for?

A man named Jim Elliot said something that rings true here: "He is no fool who gives what he cannot keep to gain what he cannot lose." Jim Elliot learned the meaning of that. A short time after he wrote those words he was killed by some of the Indians he was trying to tell about Jesus Christ. Was that a horrible death? Yes and no. It was a horrible death, because all death is horrible. But he had to die, sooner or later. We all do. And the fact that he died doing something worth dying for changed his death. In the middle of grief, his friends and family could still say his life had meaning and purpose.

Dying is one of the least skilled occupations you can find. Everybody does it, sooner or later. You can't be too dumb or too inept for it. In a sense, you could say everyone is giving his life. He's giving it to something or someone. When it's all over, they'll say, "He gave his life to science," or bowling, or drugs, or other people. Is what you're giving your life for worth it? Are you making mud pies out of your life, or something permanent and valuable? Jim Elliot died doing something ultimately worthwhile, and there is no better way to die.

The particular mode of dying isn't what's important. You can die of cancer, or die in a car accident, or die of a drug overdose. You may think that one way is a lot better or a lot worse than the others. You may be afraid of going out of this life crying and afraid and in pain. The fact is, though, that the actual experience of dying isn't so awful as you imagine it. Some ways are more painful and tedious than others, but when the actual death comes, your attention is so taken up with simple things like breathing, that it happens almost before you realize. And even if you gave the greatest deathbed performance in history, it really wouldn't change the quality of your life. The question remains, what did you give your life for?

a hunk of mud

Of course, one reason so many people are afraid to die is because they fear annihilation. You can do wonderful things all your life, and live by the right values, but you still die. You disappear. Your body rots. The people you did wonderful things for also die, and in a few years it makes very little difference whether you lived a good life or a bad life. How can life have any real meaning if that's true? Why should one way of acting be any better than another? Sooner or later we'll all die, and this universe will keep on whirling along without noticing. It's as though a bunch of infinitesimal amoebas grew in one obscure corner of the universe, flourished for a while, then disappeared again.

To a lot of people, that thought is no big deal— they tend to live on a very pragmatic level, day to day. But to someone who feels and thinks deeply, it's a shattering thought. The idea that this marvelous body of mine, these thoughts that I think and these feelings I feel are ultimately nothing more than a bunch of molecules arranged in a particular way, and that someday they will return to nothing but dirt—that's devastating. The person you love the most, the girl or guy you're infatuated with—he or she is no more significant than a hunk of mud you kick off your boots. Death, to those who don't believe in life after death, proves it. You live a while, and then you're gone—annihilated.

Those of us who believe in Jesus Christ, though, have a totally different way of looking at this. I heard it explained this way by a teacher I know. He was talking to his principal, and the principal began asking about God. My friend is a Christian, and he told what Jesus meant to him. But the principal said, "You know, I just can't believe in the kind of God you talk about when I see things happen like Viet Nam and Auschwitz."

My teacher friend said, "I think we view life a little differently, and that's why there's a conflict. He took a pencil and drew a line on a piece of paper. One end was labeled "birth" and the other "death." He said, "Correct me if I'm wrong, but I think you see life this way. It begins at birth, and it goes on for 70 years or so, and ends at death." The principal agreed that was the way he saw life.

Then my friend drew another line. It started a little to the left of the first line, and it went on and on until it ran off the page on the other side. "I see life a little differently," my friend said. "I believe it starts with conception, and goes on forever. Birth and death are merely events that happen along the way."

That's a pretty good way of summarizing the way

Christians look at eternal life. Usually when you think of heaven or hell, your thoughts are taken from a caricature of Dante's **Inferno.** You imagine some little guy running around in pajamas with a pitchfork and horns like a cow. Or you imagine a guy sitting on a cloud in a nightshirt and sandals, strumming a harp. It's really inconceivable that you would be happy there. What's there to like about that kind of heaven? You're happy going to a football game, talking to friends, making pottery. The idea that you would enjoy living in a nightshirt with a bunch of neuter people floating purposelessly in space— that's absurd! People can say, "Well, you'll be in heaven then," and if that's the kind of image it summons, it really doesn't console you much.

But what is eternal life really like? The first thing we know is what my friend was getting at by drawing his line off the page. Eternal life begins **now.** Heaven is just a continuation of the life you're living. It'll be **you** who's there—not some strange angel, but you. You'll be different in ways that we don't understand, but in many ways you'll be the same.

brownie points

One aspect of heaven and hell that particularly bothers many people is the idea of reward and punishment. You know—the people who are good get to go to heaven and live it up, while people who are bad have to go to hell and suffer. That's distasteful for a number of reasons. For one thing, I think it's hard to believe God could be totally fair, because every time our teachers or bosses or parents hand out rewards and punishments, we know there is plenty of unfairness. But even knowing God to be totally fair, heaven and hell seem embarrassing to many Christians. It seems as though the good people should be glad to sacrifice their nice position in heaven to the people in hell, if they're really as good as they're supposed to be. You can't help suspecting that the people who end up rewarded are really the same people who spend all their time in class buttering up the teacher, trying to look good. You would think that the **really** good people would be the ones who did good just to be doing good, and weren't concerned about whether they got to go to heaven at all.

But that is based on a very wrong idea of what heaven and hell are like. Heaven isn't a bunch of brownie points. That's a kind of reward which has nothing to do with what you did to deserve it. God could, if he wanted, give everyone brownie points, whether they'd been good or bad.

But there are other kinds of reward. The kind of reward you get in heaven is like the reward you get for practicing at gymnastics. The practice may be very tedious, but one day you find yourself reaping the reward—the joy of freedom of complete body control. Practicing gymnastics would be very distasteful if your only reward was having the coach give you a pat on the back. But the real reward has nothing to do with the coach. It has everything to do with what you prepared yourself for through hours of practice. That's the way the reward of heaven is, too; it's just one step beyond what you've done here on earth. It's not the end of life, but the next phase of it—a continuation and extension of what you prepared for here. And there is no way to be ready to receive those rewards but by becoming the kind of person here on earth who can appreciate and understand them.

a slice of a circle

How does our life here relate to that mysterious life beyond death? I like to think of eternal life as a huge circle, representing everything we are in the eternal dimension. Our life here is just one small slice out of that circle—a short, slightly curved line. You could never say, looking at that little slice, that it was much compared to the circle itself. Yet by measuring the curve of that little slice accurately, you can predict exactly the size and shape of the whole circle.

That's what our life here is—a tiny, insignificant slice of the total life God has for us. The way we deal with life here predicts the way our total eternal life is. That places a lot of importance on this life!

But when we get an expanded idea of what eternal life is about, then both life and death take on the proper meaning. Let's put it this way: if a guy knew he only had fifteen minutes to live, I doubt he'd spend any time on pushups. After all, pushups aren't the most pleasurable things, and there wouldn't be much point to them. But if he knew he was going to live for a long time, and that being in shape was a desirable thing, he might even find it enjoyable, because he'd be stretching and working with a goal in mind, and he could see a real point to it all. As it works out, it's nearly always true that guys who consider things from the longer point of view and do get into shape are happier than those who only think about the short-term view and end up flabby.

The same with life. When you get a glimpse of the full circle of eternal life, the values in the here and now are different. You live for what will last. Well, obviously you can't see into the future. And you can't see beyond death. But the Bible gives us some clues about eternal life. It claims to relate something of what goes on after you die, and gives true answers to the question, "What will really last?"

Certainly the Bible doesn't give a boring picture, like so many of our stereotypes. Some people make a great deal of some of the imagery the Bible uses— the Bible says the gates are pearl, the streets are gold, the foundations are made of amethyst and sapphire. I think it's meant to tell us that heaven begins where this life leaves off. When you think of the things that are most treasured and honored here, like gold and jewels, you can assume that in heaven there are far more important and beautiful things. Here, men and women dive to the bottom of the ocean and risk their lives to get pearls. There, they use them for pig iron, and make gates out of them. Here, jewels are treasured and put in precious, expensive settings. In heaven they're so common they are dumped into holes to make foundations. All the stuff men scratch and fight and slave for is no longer valuable. There are higher values. Values like love—love so fulfilled and complete we can't even dream of it here. People live there with an awareness of each other that is greater than anything we imagine here. Love will last—so you can start doing your love pushups now.

people on other planets

Another aspect of heaven I believe in is purpose. Usually, when you get the stereotyped image of heaven the biggest purpose anyone has is playing the harp. I think we'll have more purpose there than here, not less. What will our purpose be? I don't know. But it helps to speculate, just to open our minds to the kind of wild place it will be. C. S. Lewis speculated in one of his books that we might be involved in the salvation of other worlds. Perhaps we'll be messengers for God. Maybe we'll be in charge of some huge project. We don't have any way of knowing, of course; these are just guesses. But we can be quite sure that God has plans far larger than anything we would think of—and in some fantastic way we will be taking part in them. What we're doing now is preparing for that. We are getting ready. We are like athletes in training for the biggest, most important meet in history.

I find this kind of vision of heaven pretty helpful when you're afraid of death. It's a vision you can really be excited about.

There are other aspects of heaven that the Bible mentions. We're promised a body that's totally new and perfected, like Christ's body when he rose again. You feel ugly here? Not there. The most beautiful person you've ever seen will be bland in comparison to the new you.

And we will see each other there. We'll meet again, but in a new, exciting way. All the old selfishness and imperfection will be gone. Our love and caring for each other will really be complete, and we'll experience the comradeship you only feel when you are working partners in something that is demanding, exciting and beyond anything you ever dreamed you'd be capable of.

But what about hell? You can't ignore that, for it's just as plainly written about in the Bible as heaven is. We don't know much about it; we only know that those who have not listened to the voice of God, who have ignored him and gone their own way, are going to be there, and it isn't going to be a pleasant place. Once again, this bears out the seriousness of our life here. No one is going to hell for slipping up and making a few petty mistakes. Hell is for people who've lived like hell. It's the natural reward for shoving God out of your life, again and again. It's God saying, "All right, I'll leave you alone, just as you want. But I'm going to leave you totally alone." Think about it. Are you unconsciously preparing yourself for that by shoving God aside?

death and birth

"Death is a lot like birth—a little darkness, a little pain, and then a whole new world outside." Heaven doesn't remove the fear from death—death is dark, unknown and painful. But the world beyond makes the difference in overcoming that fear. You'll go into a dark passageway if you know you are going to come out into the sun at the other end. But to be thrust deeper and deeper into a pitch-black cave from which you'll never emerge—that's a terrifying thing, a thing without hope. And that is how most non-Christians think about death.

Followers of Christ know that there is a world beyond where the sun is shining and the birds are singing, and where they will know everything they always wanted to know and be everywhere they always wanted to be.

Death isn't a big scare tactic thought up by God. Its purpose isn't to paralyze us with fear so we don't do any no-no's. It's more of a cutoff date, a time when we get promoted to another kind of life. The big question is whether the way you're living now is preparing you for the promotion. Are you standing with God or against him? If the harsh reality of death prompts you to ask that question, the fear and the pain of death are worth it. For that question is the most important of all.

why don't my parents trust me?

Photo: Ed Wallowitch

Trouble with your parents?
Don't give up, man. You can train them!

When I talk to kids who have problems with parents, I nearly always begin by asking what they don't like about their parents. The answers are pretty predictable. I hear complaints again and again: (1) My parents don't trust me. (2) My parents don't love me. (3) My parents don't listen to me. (4) My parents pick on me. (5) My parents are hypocrites.

I'd be just like a parent if I told you to forget it and just do what you're told. Those problems do exist, and they're not just your fault. But they're not all your parents' fault, either. Almost anytime people have trouble getting along, it's a problem built up over a period of time. You can't say that one is at fault, or that one's innocent.

I'd like to tell you some things you can do from your end of the problem.

my parents don't trust me

A lot of kids tell me their parents don't trust them. What they usually mean is that their folks don't trust them to stay out all night, or take the family car somewhere, or choose their own friends properly. Those are things all people want to be trusted with—their own car, their own freedom, their own friends.

But how do you get to be trusted?

You have to be trustworthy, or "worthy of trust." You have to prove that you're trustworthy to your parents. That may be unfair, but that's the way it will probably be. You do it by starting with little things. If your parents tell you to get home by eleven and you're always late, they're going to say, "Well, if he can't tell time, he can't be trusted with something bigger." However, if you call from some-place and say, "Hey, Dad, I'm on my way, but it's going to take twenty-five minutes to get home, so I'll be ten minutes late," you'll find when you want some late privileges you'll have a lot better chance.

There's a good reason behind this. If your parents are smart, their goal is for you to become inde-pendent. Like birds, they don't particularly want baby birds in the nest all their lives. They want you to fly.

But to fly, you have to develop gradually. You don't go out and challenge the neighborhood cat the first day. You go out on little loops to see if you can do it. The loops get bigger and bigger, and the day may come when you're ready for the neighborhood cat. In fact, if you're really ready for something tough, your parents will enjoy it with you. To get to that stage, you have to excel at the little loops.

Break down another word: "responsibility." It's really "response ability," the ability to respond ma-turely to situations. Believe me, your parents watch how you respond to things. Can you respond to money maturely, or does it burn a hole in your pocket? When you are disappointed, do you take it in stride, or do you have to pout about it for a week? Your parents watch those things. They're not trying to spy on you; they just want to check your response ability, and see if you're ready for more.

If you really want a lot of privileges at home, I'll tell you how to get them. Just start doing all the little, dumb stuff according to the book. Stuff like making your bed, picking up your clothes and being neat, doing the dishes without being hassled into it. Do that for a while and your parents will be sitting ducks.

Think of it as a game. Parents are trainable. If you're smart, you can work them any way you want to. It's all how you think of it. Like the two mice talking about the scientist. One mouse says, "I think we've got the scientist conditioned. Every time I push this little lever he gives me food."

One other need—communication. One kid told me, "My parents don't trust me with my friends. They don't like them just because they've got long hair and they think they're troublemakers. If they knew what the kids they want me to hang out with are like, they'd be glad I have the friends I do."

"But have you ever thought of telling them?" I asked him.

How can you expect your parents to trust you with your friends unless you've told them what your friends are like? If every time they ask you a question you grunt and make them feel like it's none of their business, you're not going to get them to trust your friends.

Kids say, "My mom doesn't trust me."

"Well, why?" I ask.

"Well, she reads all the papers and hears about all the things kids are doing, and she thinks that's the kind of thing I'm doing."

"Well, does your mother know anything about you?"

"Not really."

"Why not?"

"I guess because I never told her."

Do you ever sit down and tell your parents what kind of person you really are? What you really want out of life? What your goals are, what your values are? As they see your ideas maturing, they'll feel a lot more confident to say, "He can be trusted when I'm not here."

my parents don't love me

When kids complain that their parents don't love them, I wonder how much they know about their parents.

I know what my mornings are like. Some people get up every morning and say, "Good morning, Lord." I tend to say, "Good Lord, morning."

Each morning I have conversations with the shower nozzle. From my state of semiconsciousness in the shower it looks like the only friendly thing in the world. I talk to it about my life and the day ahead. I say, "Man, I've got to go to work again, the same job I've been doing every day of my life for seventeen years. There's no way out—it's a life sentence. The kids are eating more; the rent is soaring; the more I make the more expenses seem to rise. Help!"

A million other fathers do that every day. You think your father's trapped in the corporate jungle? You're probably absolutely right.

Why does he do it? He could jump in a car, start driving, and never come back. He could desert your family and run around conceiving kids like you. That's fun, you know—no responsibilities. Just how many pleasures is your father treating himself to? Probably not too many.

So why? The only explanation that makes much sense is that he loves you, and he's determined to take care of you. Maybe he doesn't know how to show his love properly, but he does love you. His intentions are good.

What about your mom? Do you know what she's like? I'll give you some hints. First, go to the cupboard sometime and look at all the dishes. Then start with the number of days in the year. Multiply that by the meals in a day. Then multiply that by how old you are. That's roughly the number of times your mother has washed that same set of dishes. Think that gets a little boring?

Then look at your clothes. How many times has your mom washed those same sets? How many times has she folded that same T-shirt? Think that gets a little old?

Remember the smell of vomit from the first grade? Kids in the first grade are always throwing up. You could take someone blindfolded into a classroom and he could tell you nine times out of 10 it was the first grade just because of that smell. Well, think about the times you've gotten so sick you could barely make it to the john. You feel like you're going to die, and someone comes in to hold your head. Who is that? Your mother never said, "Wow, it's 2:00 AM. He'll just have to take care of it himself this time." She gets up and then, even after you've gone back to bed, she's there mopping up.

You think that's fun? Mothers aren't built so differently that they look forward to mopping up vomit at 2:00 AM. Why does she do it? Because she loves you.

my parents don't listen to me

It's amazing that people who live together for years can have such a hard time making intelligent conversation. It works both ways. You should see parents when I tell them this is a complaint kids have. They're amazed. From their point of view, it's you who won't listen to them!

Anytime you're with people who've experienced different things in life, it's hard to make good conversation. It takes creativity and effort. If you interacted with your friends like you do your parents, how many friends would you have?

Sometimes parents want to talk, but they don't know how. They ask questions nobody cares about like, "How's school?" You know how to break them of that? Sometime just tell them what school is like. Say, "Well, we got there at 8:10 and stood around waiting for the bell to ring. At 8:15 it rang and we went to home room. We sat there for half an hour and had the announcements and did this and that. Then the bell rang and we went to math. We were taught all about . . ." They'll eventually get the idea that a more creative question might help conversation.

I tell parents to try not to ask questions that can be answered simply "Yes" or "Okay." Ask questions that say, "What do you think of . . . ?" or "What is your opinion about . . . ?" The same goes for you. Try this one-week experiment. Sit down and think up five suppertime conversation topics you can involve your parents in. Then list two or three questions for each meal. "Hey, Dad, what do you think about this?" or "Mom, what's your opinion?" They'll be able to answer because everybody has an opinion. You may know more about it than they do, but you don't always have to correct them. You're not going to change them anyway. Just listen. Ask, "Why do you feel that way?" or "How did you come to this opinion?" Don't make your parents always end up in an argument with you.

A lot of kids trap their parents into logic that proves them wrong. Don't do that. All it does is get them to say "no" automatically, because they know you're trying to manipulate them.

And you should practice speaking in sentences rather than grunts. A sentence is a very easy thing, you know. You get a verb, stick a noun in front of it and you're in business. Sentences are good because they communicate thoughts. A grunt or an inflection only communicates an attitude, and you can't converse with an attitude.

Another way to get your parents to listen is to tell them once in a while that you need them. Tell them you've failed at something when you have.

I knew a guy who came within a hairbreadth of being hit by a train in the family car. He'd been careless, and it scared him half to death. He was really shook. There was no damage, but do you know what he did? He went home and told his dad about it. He didn't have to, but he did. It was his way of saying, "I make mistakes." In terms of relating to his dad, it was the smartest thing he ever did.

Writing home when you're on a trip is good, too. Even a collect phone call, within reason, won't get a complaint out of most parents. Nothing will warm a parent's heart like knowing you're a little homesick. You might be able to get along without a phone call home, or you may think, "My friends will think I'm chicken if I call." But decide what matters to you most. Do you want your parents to know that they're really loved?

my parents pick on me

I find that a lot of "picking on me" is really caused by a lack of information. Parents want to know what's going on in their kids' lives. A lot of times kids don't volunteer it. What can a parent do but pick on you?

Maybe your parents are always picking on you about your friends because they don't know what kind of people they are. If Susie Jones, the girl your mother thinks you should take out, is a hypocrite, sit down and explain that.

Kids complain their parents pick on them about school. The trouble is, they haven't told them enough about school. Once you volunteer information, the picking will let up.

You can eliminate some kinds of picking by figuring out what petty things bother them. What irritates your dad? Maybe it's that you slouch at the table, or he doesn't like your hair in your eyes. Well, is it worth it? Is it worth all those hassles every day for the next two or three years? If you know he gets irritated when you don't respond the first time to something he says, why not just give in and respond right away? Sometimes I think kids try to start a war with their parents. It's not worth it.

Sometimes there are real reasons why your parents pick on you. Did you ever ask them why they care so much about what kind of clothes you wear? It might be that some of the things they say have some reasons. Is it possible that your mother knows something about life that makes her think twice about short skirts? You might try asking her.

One other cause of your parents' picking on you —your independence. Some parents don't understand you're trying to get away from that formless blob called "family" and become an independent person. Your parents probably don't understand why you're tired of being so-and-so's son or daughter. They think you don't like it because you don't like them—they don't understand that you're just trying to find your own identity.

When you just want to be alone in your room, they think it's because you don't like them. When you don't feel like going where the rest of the family is going, they think it's because you're rejecting them. When you want to move out and get an apartment, they think it's because you can't stand to be in the same house with them. That hurts them, so they pick on you. But try explaining that you're trying to become an individual. Sit down and explain to them as patiently as possible that you love them, but that you have to be known for what you are, not for what they are. It may take them a while, but I think they'll be able to understand that, especially if you lace it liberally with the statement that you love them and enjoy them. A lot of parents picking on their kids are grasping for some kind of assurance of your acceptance. You want them to stop picking on you? Try giving them the assurance.

my parents are hypocrites

I was riding on an airplane, next to a kid in sandals and blue jeans. I started talking to him, and pretty soon I found out he was down on his dad. His parents were total hypocrites, highly involved in the oppressive corporate structure, wrapped up in possessions.

I said, "How come you're flying in this airplane?"

He said it was the fastest way to get where he wanted. I also found out that he paid the bill with a travel card his father had given him.

Now, I don't understand that. Granted, plenty of adults are hypocrites. But who was flying in the airplane? If you're walking across the country eating berries on the way, I respect that. I like the Walden Pond idea. I like the thought of pitching a tent by the creek and eating roots and frogs. That's honest, that's back to the earth, and it appeals to me. We need some of that. But don't tell me about your folks' hypocrisy when your own life is full of it.

Kids say their parents live in a society that doesn't

respect people, where corporate monsters devour people. I won't argue with that. But I ask them: "Are you using your parents? Do you see them as saps you should walk on, or slaves that take care of your clothes? If so, I'm more interested in hearing you talk about how you're going to change your own life."

parents are lonely

Most of what I'm saying is this: let's be fair to parents. Let's be at least as fair to them as you would be to anyone you met at school. You know how unsure you feel when you get around a group of people you don't know? Well, that's how parents feel around high school kids. They don't know quite how to act. Do you blame them?

I try to make some assumptions about everybody I meet. I think you can apply them to your parents, too, because they are people.

(1) I always assume that everyone I meet is lonely. I won't always be right, but I'll be right about 90 percent of the time.

(2) I assume everybody is frightened and inse-cure, so I try to do things that won't threaten them.

What would it do to your relationship if you made those assumptions with your parents? What if you made a special point of being nice when they were busy or wound up over something? What if you gave them a compliment once in a while? Try going over to your mother some night when she's doing the dishes and giving her a hug, not to try to get something out of her, but just to say you love her. I'll tell you, the little warm shivers will go up and down her spine.

Lovers do things for each other just because they want to—not because they hope to get something out of it. It just makes them feel good to do it. Did it ever occur to you to do that at home?

There's a scriptural principle here. It's expressed beautifully in the famous prayer of St. Francis of Assisi, who said, "Grant that I may not so much seek . . . to be loved as to love." Do you like that just because it's sentimental? Real love isn't sentimental. You'll learn that if you try to practice it at home. But it does bring happiness, because the only way to get real happiness is to give it away.

problem parents

Occasionally parents have deep problems. Most parents, I'm convinced, really love their kids and want to help them, not bug them. But there are exceptions, and of course every parent has faults of some kind. How do you handle that?

Suppose your dad had only one leg. Would you be angry if he wouldn't run races with you? Not a chance. Well, suppose your dad or mom has been crippled psychologically by certain things in his youth. Are you going to hold it against him because, say, he was raised in a home where discipline was administered unwisely and he picked up the wrong signals, and now he overdoes it with you? If your mom overreacts, could it be because sometime in her life something happened to make her fearful, something she'd never be able to talk about with you?

Will Rogers said he never met a man he didn't like. He didn't say that because all his life he had the incredible good luck to meet only great people. He meant that if you get to know a person well enough, you can like him, and you can accommodate the flaws. That's true of parents, too. Why look only at the negatives? If they were somebody else's parents, you'd probably think they were interesting characters.

What's more, there's the possibility of learning from them. Most people learn from positive examples, and that's certainly the easiest. But there is another possibility—to learn from a negative example.

I know of a pair of guys who were brought up in a terrible family situation. Their parents were fighting constantly, threatening divorce. The two sons took very different paths. One got all involved in the situation: he'd get in the middle of a fight, or take one side or the other. And the cycle got him. You see, no matter how much you dislike your parents now, you'll find yourself acting just like them unless you do something about it. That's one of the worst things about a bad home—it creates a cycle that doesn't stop with one generation. That son ended up making the same tragic mistakes his parents had.

The other son, however, broke the cycle. He didn't get involved in the fights; he backed away and he did his own thing. He was helpful when he could be, but primarily when things got bad, he backed off. Today he's as together as you can imagine.

Why? Because he worked at learning from a bad situation. Okay, your father is a drunk or your mother is an addict, or your folks are always fighting. It's a problem that can't be solved overnight, and if they don't want to solve it, it won't be solved. You're stuck with it, at least until you're eighteen and can make a life of your own.

But don't spend all your time blaming your parents. They're crippled in some ways; the best you can do is be kind. Just say to yourself, "When I get married I'm going to be a little more careful to find the right kind of mate." Or, "When I have a son I'm going to be a better listener than my dad is." That's tough to be successful at. It takes a lot of maturity. But it can be done.

It's tough to have a good relationship with your parents. Very few people can be completely successful at it. But it can make a tremendous difference in your life. Few things are closer to you emotionally than your parents. When things are bad at home, everything's affected. But when things are good at home, life's a lot better.

what do I do
when my parents fight?

Not everyone worries about his parents' fighting. But if you do, the problems seem insurmountable.

Do you know what it's like to lie in bed at night, listening to your parents fight? Have you lived with the gnawing worry that your parents were going to split up? It's a terrible feeling. Everything you consider secure turns into sponge—you can't put any weight on it. It can make you feel hopeless and lost like nothing else. Because nobody—not your friends, not your teachers, not your brothers and sisters—has the power to affect you like your parents.

Chances are you aren't constantly paranoid about this. In your home, though everything may not be perfect, and there are probably awkward times when your parents do fight, there's no real doubt things will hold together.

But when your parents fight, the problems are all you can think about. Food gets tasteless when you eat too many meals with a family that's feuding. Sleep gets troubled when you wake to hear loud voices. Peace of mind is hard to find when you're caught in the middle of a fight between two people you love in a deep way. And what can you do?

jumping onstage with Hamlet

I suggest you move out of the play and into the theater wings, where you can watch your parents as though they were actors on the stage. Then you can apply the lessons you learn.

Let's say I go to see a production of **Hamlet.** I'm sitting in the audience, and I get very emotionally involved with the production. The play really comes to life. When it comes down to the last scene, where everyone gets killed, I leap up on the stage and try to throw myself between the actors. Or maybe I sit tight, but when I leave the theater I'm so worked up I go out and stab people too. I think you could fairly say I was making a bad response to the play. The best way to handle **Hamlet** is to sit and watch the play and leave the theater thinking about it.

Yet, if your parents are really having trouble, your first reaction is to get involved in the fight. You want to leap up onstage and throw yourself between them. But that's a bad impulse. You're too minor a character. There are people, clergymen and coun- selors and relatives, who need to come onstage and help their friends. But you can't.

Your second reaction is to go out and, inflamed by what's happened at home, start acting just like your parents. Start stabbing your friends right and left. But obviously that's a bad idea too.

The best plan is to sit tight and stay out of things. It's rough, because you can't leave the theater— the emotions onstage really get to you. But if you realize that you don't have to live with this thing for your whole life, but only a few more years, you can grit your teeth and learn from it. The lesson may be invaluable later on.

clear the air?

Of course, there is a point where you can help. You can express your feelings, and clear the air between you and your parents. You might be able, through that, to help your parents realize how serious their fighting is. But you can't solve their problems for them. If you try you may get crushed in the middle of forces you're not strong enough to master. You should carry your end as well as possible—try not to mouth off, try to understand their problems, try to be pleasant. But you're not a family counselor. You can't sit them down and say, "Come on, Dad, we've got to straighten things out." Good or bad, whenever your parents look at you they see you in your diapers. They can't imagine any smart advice coming out of you.

So you aren't generally going to single-handedly straighten out your family's problems. The most important thing is to keep your own head screwed on straight.

But with all your emotions churning, how can you do that? Here are some general principles I'd suggest:

(1) Never take sides. That isn't going to be easy, because in any situation it will appear to you that one side is right and the other wrong. But when you get very far into a fight, you nearly always discover that there really are two sides.

Say your dad comes home from work acting very irritable. Your mother says something and he over-reacts. It develops into a fight. You might think, "Dad has no right to jump on her that way." But there may be a number of hidden factors you don't know about. For one thing, you don't know the kind of pressure he's been under all day.

I remember a guy giving me a quick tour of the main office of a big insurance firm. He showed me how things are structured. There are lots of little desks out in the middle of a room where everything a guy says can be listened to. He moves up a step and they put a little partition around him, but his head and feet still show. A little higher and they cover his feet. One step above that they cover his head with a little glass divider. Above that he gets a room without a door, and eventually he gets a door. Then it comes down to the furniture. He or she begins with a Formica desk and imitation paneling, and then a real wood desk and real paneling. Then he gets two buttons on his phone. Eventually he gets a secretary outside his office.

The thing is so structured that you can go see anyone, and just by looking around the office, you know where he or she stands. You know who's considered a good employee.

Now in that structure your dad may feel tremendous pressures. He may be watching younger friends get laid off. He may be worried about being out of a job at forty years old. And all that may be involved in his getting irritated at home.

"Well," you say, "it's not my mom's fault." But that isn't how a married couple looks at problems. If he's under that kind of pressure, your mom ought to be helping him cope. Maybe she's not holding up her end that way. Then again, maybe she's coping with pressures you don't understand—perhaps she's trying to figure out how to be seen as a person with value and a housewife at the same time.

Or there might be any number of other factors.

Perhaps they're having sexual problems. How are you going to know about that? There are too many factors for you to even think about taking sides intelligently. Even if you could, taking sides wouldn't help. The nature of family problems is that if you go around trying to determine who's to blame and who isn't, you don't help anything. The blamed party feels guilty or angry, and the blameless party feels self-righteous. To find a solution, you have to have determined action by both parties.

(2) Accept your parents, weaknesses and all. You can't do that if you believe in the prevalent American myth of the well-rounded person. There simply aren't any well-rounded people. Everybody has a bad side, a weak side. Everyone has needs, and that's why working together is such an important aspect of Christianity. We complement each other. If there were well-rounded people, they wouldn't need complementing.

So when looking at your parents, don't go looking for their faults. Look for their strengths. One person may have an excellent ability to love and accept, while another person's abilities lie in organization. Believe me, they're both essential; one isn't "better" than the other.

(3) Be realistic. Remember, first of all, that all families go in cycles. There are times when your parents are under a lot of pressure. Don't freak out because one week is bad. Things sometimes get bad in the normal course of events, but they also get better.

(4) Don't compare. It doesn't help to try com-

paring your own family with others. You may think a certain girl's dad is really nice when you're there, and you wish your own father were like that. But you can't compare. You see her dad only in a good light—he's not going to spout off while you're around. He's in a totally different role with you— for instance, he's not in charge of disciplining you. So naturally he comes off a little differently.

Besides, families are different. How your parents act toward each other depends on their own backgrounds. Certain ethnic groups tend to express themselves more. Maybe you're from an Italian family, and your parents argue loudly. You go to a high school with a lot of kids from English or Scandinavian backgrounds, and you wish like crazy for the peace and quiet you find in their homes. Okay, wish all you want. But don't go thinking that their homes are necessarily better just because they express themselves differently. Maybe that calmness is covering a feud. A silent feud is worse than an argument any day.

So don't just watch the arguments. Watch for the kissing, the loving and forgiving. If your dad loses his temper and yells at your mom, but the next thing you know they're cooing and cuddling, and you're the fifth of eight kids—relax. It's just their style to yell. And if you don't see overt signs of affection between your parents, it's not necessarily because they don't love each other. People have different styles of expressing love. Some people come from homes where love isn't expressed by talking or touching. It's expressed by duty. Like in **Fiddler on**

the Roof: "Whaddya mean, do I love you? I wash your socks, milk the cow, have your children. Of course I love you."

desperate and panicked

I suppose the most common reaction to problems between your parents is anxiousness. Your parents are fighting, and it gets to you. You lie awake at night listening to them fight, and a cold shadow creeps over your life. Everything that means warmth and security is falling apart. You're sinking.

That helpless feeling is something you can't fight against. Fighting directly against it is like fighting quicksand; you only wear yourself out, and you get deeper and deeper into it. It can really hurt you. It can make you paranoid and afraid. It can make you talk too much or clam up with your problems.

But it can also teach you some extremely valuable lessons. First of all, when you think of how desperate and panicked those feelings of helplessness can be, think about your parents' feeling exactly the same way. They probably do. They are already straining with anxiety over growing old. Most people are very frightened of middle age and old age. They realize how vulnerable they are economically. At that age, what does happen to you if you lose your job? And then the frustrations of marriage, which they probably thought would be their dream-come-true, add to that. They are going to be living with those problems the rest of their lives, while you just have to survive two or three more years.

You're probably just one of a family of anxiety-ridden people. Realize that and you'll be able to empathize with your parents. You may be able to talk to them better, understand them better. You may even find yourself feeling sorry for them, which in small doses isn't all bad.

But your feelings of anxiety can do even more for you; they may drive you to the rock bottom of security. I like to think of life as a system of bonuses. The only thing that absolutely cannot fail you, no matter how rotten you are or how rotten the world is, is God's love. Everything on top of that is a wonderful bonus. Maybe you have one friend in the world. That may seem bad, but actually that one friend is a precious bonus. You weren't guaranteed any. Or maybe you're a person who is doing well in school, and you're going to get the education you need and get a good job. That's a bonus, too. Maybe you've got a very steady temperament, and your emotions don't soar up and down every five minutes. That's a bonus. All the things in life are bonuses, and they ought to be thought of that way. The only thing that isn't a bonus, but is your base pay, is "God loves you."

Everything else may be stripped away. Look at our world. Ten years ago, what was more sure than gas to run your car? Yet now the Arabs say if we use oil at the rate it was used in 1973, it'll all be gone in forty-five years. What was more stable to us than oil and coal and minerals, the very substance of the earth? Yet now we can't take them for granted.

Friends can be stripped away. The security of a home can be stripped away. Warmth and food can be taken away. Your own mental stability can go out the window. The only genuinely sure thing is God. "He will keep in perfect peace all those who trust in him, whose thoughts turn often to the Lord" (Isa. 26:3). We like to live believing in the stability of other things. But ultimately we need to push our roots down deep enough to realize this is our only true stability.

Instead of letting anxiety about your parents drive you into a frenzy, you should allow it to drive you deeper into God's grace. Only when you've done this, and the love you get at home is truly a bonus to you—an "extra" for which you're thankful—can you really cure anxiety.

the big split

Increasingly, problems between parents are going into court, and ending in divorce. Thousands of kids have to cope with their parents' separation or divorce every year. Maybe you're one of them. Maybe you're going to be one of them. Or maybe you just worry that you're going to be one of them.

It may help to know that it's not the end of the world. It can be very, very bad, but even at the worst it is the kind of thing you can live through.

Most of the principles for surviving a divorce are the same as those for surviving parental fights. You are going to want to take sides, and in some cases your parents will try to drag you into it. It's only natural for you to feel that one person is right and the other wrong, whether you have an accurate picture or not.

I would caution you, however, to maintain objectivity as much as possible, particularly by loving both parents. If you show a spirit of forgiveness, it'll be easier for your parents to do the same.

Often, too, it gets kind of tedious living with one parent. That parent has to be all things to you, while the other parent only comes in once in a while and treats you to nice things. Try consciously not to glamorize the parent you don't live with, and don't verbally compare the two of them. There are enough wounds between them without your flicking the scab off.

You may feel—many do—that the divorce or separation was your fault. Well, it is possible that you had some small part in it. It couldn't have been a very large part, but you may have contributed somewhat. There is no point, however, in trying to feel constant remorse for this. You may be tempted to live over your faults and mistakes repeatedly, as though that would help. But you can't pay for your past. You can't make up for it by suffering. The only solution to personal sins is to ask forgiveness of God, and accept it. Live in the present, thanking God for dealing with your past through Jesus Christ.

walking on crutches

At the same time, you need to become more aware of yourself, especially living with only one parent. A daughter raised by her mother doesn't have a father figure. She may find that she needs strong, father-image guys, and she likes to be touched and cuddled. Maybe she falls in love with older guys, teachers, youth pastors. It may help to realize why you're that way—you are searching for a father image. Realize it, and compensate for it. Find some person you can trust, someone who will understand, someone without any ulterior motives (that's pretty important for a girl—problems do come up). Sure, that person is a crutch, but if you have a broken leg you need a crutch.

Same thing for a guy. A dominating mother is a genuine problem. If you find yourself not particularly enjoying the company of other guys, there is some possibility you secretly hate your father for hurting your mother. Latent homosexuality is thought by some to be tied to this. An outside adult can often be helpful. Adults are usually much more open to being a friend to you than you'd think at first; in fact, most would welcome it.

Older brothers and sisters can also be a very important bridge. They may have a far deeper understanding of the problems that led to the divorce; talking to them can help. If you're an older brother or sister, I think you ought to be particularly sensitive to ways you can heal the pain in your younger brothers and sisters. Just talking things out can be tremendously healing.

non-negotiable demands

One other thing comes to mind. If your parents are having problems, make sure you're not contributing to them. You can create friction by putting up big demands that, say, strain your parents' finances (a lot of fighting is over money). You've got to have a ten-speed, because everybody does. Or you put a strain on your mother's time when you know she's busy. Your parents want to please you, but your demands can really paint them into a corner. And sometimes the way you relay what one parent said to you to the other is nothing but nasty politicking. If you want a peaceful home, you have to help create it. That may require giving up some of the things you want in order to preserve peace. The unwillingness to give anything up for another's good is one of the biggest problems of any marriage —and you're a part of the equation.

the oyster

You know how an oyster makes a pearl? A pearl begins with some kind of irritation coming into the life of the oyster—a grain of sand, or a piece of shell. Instead of trying to expel the irritation, which an oyster can't do anyway, the oyster surrounds it with its own body fluids and gradually encases it with a smooth, beautiful coating.

Extreme problems like troubled parents can have the same effect on us. You can try to ignore them, put them out of your life, react violently to them, but it doesn't work out. If, however, you surround them with love and understanding, gaining personal applications to your own future, you may end up with something infinitely valuable. You may develop a personal character that will take you through life stronger, able to help others. It may be that God has a future need for a great number of people who know how it feels to be a child from a troubled home.

does prayer

change anything?

You feel battered, exhausted and thoroughly unsettled.
Whom can you go to?

A few days ago I drove home from a meeting feeling roughly as though I had been caught in a washing machine. Facing a series of deep and agonizing problems, I felt battered, exhausted and thoroughly unsettled. The minute I fought free of one problem, another hit me in the face like a wet undershirt. Yet I couldn't stop struggling or I would drown.

Riding home alone, I began to think about what I needed. I decided I only wanted solitude. I wanted time to find myself. I'd have liked to ask somebody to join me, but for the life of me I couldn't think who. I needed a friend closer than a brother, someone who simply wouldn't leave me or give up on me, no matter what. I needed a place where all the complex problems could come into perspective and be sorted out.

And where do I find that kind of place, and that kind of friend? The only place I can find it is with God. He is a friend who will never leave me or forsake me. He knows me intimately. He sees the future, and He knows exactly how my personal dilemmas will work out. He puts everything into perspective; the things I see as overwhelming look fairly trivial from his perspective. Most of all, he loves me. **Loves!**

So what do I do? Do I take out a pencil and paper, make a list of all my problems, and then ask God to solve each one? No, that's not really what I need. My problems go deeper, and so must their solution. I need a relationship with God himself. And if I think about a relationship strictly as something I profit from, it isn't a relationship. A guy who claims to love a girl, yet only talks to her to get her in bed, to get some pleasure from her, doesn't know much about relationships or about love. Yet that is exactly how most of us are tempted to talk to God.

an insensitive God?

Prayer is getting in touch with God on an intimate, personal basis. Shutting your eyes may help; many people find it does. But staring out of a window or taking a walk may help, too. That doesn't make it less prayerful.

We all have misconceptions about prayer we need to get rid of. First, prayer isn't trying to get an insensitive God to be sensitive. We all act as if it were at times, though. "Dear God, I'm terribly concerned about the people in Bangladesh. I really feel their pain. I wanted to point out their situation to you." A popular song sounds like this: "What the world needs now/Is love, sweet love. . . . Lord, if you really want to know." But God doesn't need our instructions in loving. The real God is infinitely sensitive and compassionate.

Nor is prayer trying to get a forgetful God to remember. We get the idea that if we get really emotional, or raise our voices, or assume a certain posture or way of holding our hands, or use polysyllabic religious words over and over, God, who is slightly deaf, will hear us and remember the thing he forgot. But God isn't like that.

Finally, prayer is not trying to make an unwilling God willing. That idea sounds like this: God's got all this power saved up, with which he could cure all the leukemia patients in the world just as easily as you flip a lock of hair out of your face. So I'm going to beg him until he'll do it. He's kind of lazy, and he doesn't like to use his power very often, so I've got to keep pulling on him and begging until he heals my father or my grandfather. There is a place for persistence in prayer, but this nagging goes beyond persistence. It assumes an unwilling God you can bully into something.

All these kinds of prayer are disqualified because they don't match up with what we know is true of God. He is absolutely loving, absolutely concerned.

baseball and bangladesh

In order to find out what prayer really should be, we need to think first about what I label "larger concerns." Suppose I want to play a baseball game, and I'd rather not have to play it in the rain. So I get together with a group of my friends and pray that it doesn't rain.

However, twenty miles away there is a farmer whose family and livelihood depend on corn growing, and corn has to have rain. In fact, the whole cereal crop for the entire world depends on the right amount of rain. Yet I think I can jump in and twist God's arm to let me play my game.

And actually, God's concerns are even larger than that. He is concerned about people starving, but apparently there are things even more significant than that—things like the way God comes into a human heart humbly and without force. Right now we are seeing thousands starve. Yet God doesn't directly intervene. Why not? One reason is that if we saw God constantly working miracles every time someone were hungry, it would blind us to the more subtle qualities of his love. He would be nothing but a big miracle machine. So apparently God's larger concerns make him normally feed the earth through indirect means like farmers, instead of personally and miraculously. He doesn't want to dazzle us; he wants us to love him voluntarily. It's a larger concern I doubt any of us would even think of. Yet God holds it constantly in mind. I think about my baseball game; he's concerned about people in India and about the whole way he's working in history.

James 4:3 says the reason we don't get what we ask for is because we ask with the wrong motives— "you want only what will give **you** pleasure." If my prayers are narrow, concerned only with myself and not with the larger concerns of the world, God isn't going to respond to them. God's vision extends beyond my horizons.

Another facet of prayer I find important to think about is what I call the "flip side" of prayer. I know the result I'm looking for when I pray, but is there an unseen side? If all my prayers were answered just the way I prayed them what would be the result? Is the result something that is in line with God's overall plan?

Suppose a tornado is roaring across a field toward my house. I pray, "God, protect me. Wipe out my neighbor's house if you have to, but supernaturally intervene to protect me and my house."

If God answers me and the tornado hops over my house, or takes a sudden detour and goes around my property line, I'd no doubt be grateful to him. (Though if the tornado detoured through my neighbor's property, he might not be as thrilled as I.)

But suppose that kind of prayer were answered every time I got into trouble. Suppose whenever I went into a skid on an icy road, I could pray for help and the laws of physics and chemistry would be violated, making my tires supernaturally grip the road. And every time there's a natural disaster, I would get out of it. Every time I would start getting sick, I would pray and suddenly I would be well again. My friends, too, would seem to have miraculous cures from cancer and other diseases. Those are nice things, but is there a flip side? I think there is. After a while, I think, my neighbors would start muttering to themselves. They might want to get on my good side so they wouldn't get cancer. But on the other hand, they'd wonder about me. I'd be a little inhuman to them.

plastic-sealed, problem-proof

Now suppose all Christians learned to pray the way I did, so that everything we asked for we got. Soon the Christians would be the people nothing bad ever happened to. Other people would die of starvation, but Christians wouldn't. Other people would have tragedies in their family, but Christians wouldn't. I suspect that if that happened, Christians wouldn't be terribly popular. We'd be a separate race, a race that does not have to live under the natural laws that govern the hostility of our planet. People who lacked our advantage would resent us.

And it would go in diametric opposition to God's plan. The reason Jesus came to earth was to join the human race, not escape it. As his followers, we too are to share the hurts and sorrows of other people. Jesus did work miracles to remove some of those hurts, and he does today. But miracles are always exceptions. If they were everyday, normal occurrences, we wouldn't call them miracles. Exceptions aside, Jesus didn't invite us all to leave the real world and join some Magic Kingdom where there are no problems. His idea was that, facing the world just as other people face it, we'd learn to transcend or transform those problems with his power. Jesus said we are the salt of the earth. If salt doesn't get mixed in with the food it's supposed to season, it is useless. We too are supposed to mix up with all the confusion and problems of the human race, and transform them through God's presence in us. But if we could make God turn us into a plastic-sealed, problem-proof race, we'd have lost all our ability to communicate the message Jesus brought to the world.

The "I'm special" mentality is always repulsive to people. If it is always possible for me to coerce God into healing a friend of mine from leukemia, then the question has got to be raised, why in the world can't I get God concerned enough to heal the whole cancer ward? He doesn't come down to heal the whole hospital, so he must be either a God who plays favorites, or a God who has limited power—

he can only do one zap a day, and he's already used it on me.

Not only would that mentality alienate you from your neighbors, but it would eventually make your relationship with God flippant. Prayer would be something you use to control God, like magic. It'd be a plaything. God would become a machine. You'd have to punch all the buttons in the right combinations to make him work.

So when I pray, I need to think about the flip side of prayer. What happens if I really get my way with God, not just this time, but every time?

a junior Merlin

Actually, I don't think the primary purpose of prayer is getting God to do things at all. I believe that prayer is the process of getting to know God. It isn't God who changes when I pray; it's me. I get my knowledge, my desires, my will and my thoughts in tune with his, so that we really become one. Gradually I find that I want the same things God wants for this world, and I'm willing to allow him to use me to bring about those things.

Now most people really aren't interested in that kind of prayer. They're not terribly interested in changing themselves or getting to know God. They'd rather have a magic show. They are interested in being junior Merlins. All they see in the Bible is miracles; it's a kind of **Ripley's Believe It or Not.** They want to be able to decide things for God, like who should live or die, who should be healed, who shouldn't, whose farm should be destroyed, whose baseball game should be rained out, whose football team should win, which heavyweight champion should knock out the brains of the other. You can tell that's what they want out of prayer, because the more they get their way with God, the better they like praying. They enjoy the power. Essentially, they would rather be God themselves than allow God to be God.

But being a junior Merlin is not ultimately satisfying. There is a basic human desire to control things, but it isn't the most basic. The most basic need is to know God, to let his personality and his presence fill your life. It's a hunger so deep, so gnawing, that if you let it to the surface of your life it can almost overcome you. Mostly we keep it hidden, even from ourselves. But I suspect every one of us wants to know God on an intimate level, and wants it far more than any other thing we've ever prayed for.

Many people seem to think that becoming a Christian means automatically having that deep, intimate level of peace with God. Actually, asking Jesus Christ to enter your life is more like an introduction. When you're introduced to someone, you may go away with goose pimples of excitement, or you may feel "So what?" But regardless of your feelings, you don't "know" that person . . . not yet, anyway. The same with Christ. If you've accepted him into your life, you've got the introduction, but there is a lot of growing to go in your relationship.

There is no more comfortable, warm, pleasurable place in the world than near to the heart of God.

Prayer leads you there. I find that much richer than a strictly functional approach to prayer. With a functional approach, you have a washer to wash your clothes, a dryer to dry your clothes, a refrigerator to keep your food cold, aspirin to cure your headache and God to take care of any problems you can't solve with one of the preceeding things. God goes around finding parking places, keeping your parents from being mad at you, bringing instant recall on tests so that while other kids in your class are rewarded for preparation, memory and ability, you can come in without preparation, pray a simple prayer and hit the top of the curve. That's what a lot of people want, but it's not something deeply worthwhile.

miracles

Now of course God does sometimes intervene in history, and there are miracles. I have seen some, and even if I hadn't, I would only have to read the New Testament to know they exist. We are told in the New Testament to pray for the sick and to ask God for the things we really need. That is a long way, however, from thinking that every time I close my eyes and talk to God about something it should work out just the way I want it to. Instead, at the same time I am talking to God about something, I should be trying to understand what he wants in that situation. I should be trying to align myself with what he wants.

When I pray, I say, "This is what I want, Lord, and what seems best to me. But I know I'm limited.

You do what's right and I'll be happy. Thy will be done."

There are some Christians who would say that's wrong. They think I'm giving God a back door out— that I'm showing a lack of faith. I respect them as Christians, but I believe they're wrong about this. I don't think God wants or needs a back door out. I do, however. I want to be able to talk sincerely and frankly to God, telling him just how I feel about situations I care about. Yet I want to let him run the show. I don't want to put up a nonnegotiable demand that isn't the very best thing from his all-seeing, all-knowing point of view.

Do I pray for people? Of course I do. The Bible tells us to. But I don't see praying for people as straightening out God as to what they need. I see it as agonizing beside God over a fellow human being who is in pain. I happen to believe that God sits on the edge of every sick bed in the world, wanting to move in and cure that person. When I pray, I sit beside him, agonizing with him. Often he does heal; most sick people in our society do get well, often with the help of doctors whose wisdom and ability ultimately come from God. But there are many times when God does not intervene, and when the laws of the universe which he created take their course. That doesn't happen because God likes pain and death. It doesn't happen because no one has come up with the right prayer, and so God can't do anything. It happens because there are more important things in God's view of the universe than whether that person recovers to live another ten or twenty years to die of some other disease. The overarching scheme of God's work is to work through the human heart, not through flashy miracles.

Some will object, "But doesn't your kind of prayer leave out faith?" But it seems to me the facts are the other way around. Is faith in the strength and fervor and "rightness" of my prayers? Then it's in something that doesn't really deserve the absolute confidence of faith—me. I know myself well enough to question my motives and my ideas about the world. Faith is faith in God, or it isn't faith at all. It is faith that God knows what he is doing, and that he is taking care of us, no matter how desperate things seem to be.

an anti-puke prayer

It's not that prayer lacks benefits.

There are tremendous benefits to letting yourself just be with God in your prayers—to think his thoughts, and listen to his words, and tell him your own feelings, and hold up people and situations to him when you know they need his help. There is tremendous peace that comes with the sense of oneness with God. There is tremendous excitement knowing that you are cooperating with God's will, and your life is going to mean something because you're tied up with God's goals.

When you meet God in prayer, you are meeting someone who loves you in a far greater sense than any boyfriend or girlfriend ever will. That, not what you can get out of it, should be your motivation in going to him.

Naturally, the greed motive is going to slip in. Just a few weeks ago I had a very bad case of the flu. All I could do was puke, and as I hung my head over the edge of the toilet I was crying out to God to help me stop throwing up. I don't think God minds that, though it is somewhat selfish. Now that I'm well, I'm not praying for other people who are puking. But he understands my weaknesses. And he wants to hear me expressing my deepest thoughts.

But he also wants me to grow. That's why, at the very same time I was crying to God, I was also saying, "If there's value in this, or something I need to learn, I'm willing to be sick." And I did realize that there might be value just in being sick exactly the way other human beings are. I'm human, and I understand human weakness because I experience it. My neighbor can't say, "Well, Jay has an anti-puke prayer; nothing bad ever happens to him. The minute he gets sick he just sends up this prayer that makes him well. So Jay could never really understand me and my doubts and frustrations, because he doesn't have any."

the opposite sex and God

Prayer, like any other kind of relating, takes time to learn. If you're getting to know a member of the opposite sex, conversation often starts out pretty awkwardly. Then too, after you've known that person for a while the initial excitement tends to wear off. Talking gets kind of boring. Only when you've known someone for a long time is conversation effortless and relaxed. Relating to God is exactly the same.

It can be awkward at first, and the initial excitement does tend to wear off.

The only prescription that works for everybody is persistence. It works in human relationships: if you spend time regularly together, talking honestly or doing things, you're going to develop a deep sense of unity. The same with God. It's often hard to talk to him: you feel as though you're wasting time, you get nervous, you get bored and your concentration on what you're saying (or what he's saying) flees. It's natural, so don't be upset when it comes. But don't give up.

I'd say the first grade in the school of prayer is setting aside one special time of talking to God and doing some inspirational reading, either in the Bible or some other Christian book. Many people find it's best to do it the first thing in the morning; others function better in the evening. Sometimes a study hall, if you can get some privacy, is the ideal time. The only really essential ingredient is quiet, and if you have to take a walk to find it, that's fine.

The graduate school of prayer is, I believe, "prayer without ceasing"—that is, constant prayer as the day goes on. I don't mention this to make you give up on the idea of one time set aside for God—you have to go through elementary school to get to graduate school. But you can begin to take some graduate courses while you're in the lower grades. Try, as your day goes on, to be aware of God. Try to remember his presence when you're faced with a problem, or when you feel angry or worthless. When you feel good, remember to thank him. Treat him as a friend walking by your side.

This kind of prayer will bring you closer to the God who is really worth knowing. He is not a push-button God. He is not a God you are trying to get on your side. You are trying to learn to be on his side. You are trying to learn to adopt his principles, his ideas, his understanding and knowledge. Prayer is one of the primary ways to grow to know him.

why obey anybody?

**Teachers, cops, parents, bosses—they're wrong sometimes.
Why should you obey them?**

Here's a typical scene: you've barely started talking on the telephone when your mother starts getting on you for talking so long. She makes you hang up. You get into an argument. Somewhere in the middle of that argument you realize your sister was on the phone just before you were, and your mother probably heard that and thought it was you. She thinks you've been on the phone all that time. It's too late for that fact to calm things down, though; she's furious at you for talking back, and you go storming out of the room with her yelling at you. Later on you have all kinds of mixed feelings. You feel guilty for mouthing off to your mother, but on the other hand, you know she was wrong. So why should you obey her?

There are similar scenes played out every day in thousands of homes. They bring up a conflict with authority: the parents are supposed to rule the home, but often you'd rather they didn't. The same thing goes on at school between students and teachers. Conflicts between the government and individual citizens come up every time someone gets caught speeding or taking drugs. When you're working and the boss tells you to do something you hate doing, you feel a surge of rebellion. Or how about when there's something you want to do, yet you know God would not want you to? That's another conflict.

There are innumerable sources of authority in your life, constantly telling you what to do. You certainly don't have to feel guilty over rebellious feelings, because they're normal. But when it comes to authority, Christians find most of the time that their duty is to obey. That's one of the most unpopular parts of Christianity. Just about everybody thinks Jesus was a neat person, worth imitating. But when they reach the part of the Bible that says, "Submit yourself to the earthly authorities," they balk.

That's because freedom is a very popular theme. Everybody wants to be free, and a common popular assumption is that the way to be free is to do only what you feel like. "Don't let anyone box you in with his ideas of what you should do. Do **your** thing." The fewer inhibitions you have and the fewer people you have to obey, the freer you are.

i could run my own life

I think we have to reject that. Christians see freedom not as freedom from authority—in which case a wild dog would be freer than any of us—but freedom to do what will ultimately satisfy us in life. That freedom very often comes as a result of being under authority—especially under one particular authority.

We Christians give ultimate authority to one man only—Jesus Christ. That's really what Christianity is all about. We pray something like this: "Listen God, I could run my own life, or let it be run according to what my teachers want or what my friends think is good. But I know that won't work. I want you to be the authority. I want you to be Lord in my life." That is the basic step in coming to know Jesus as a person. Authority is definitely part of being a Christian.

There's more to it than Christ's authority, though.

There are other authorities in our lives—our parents, our teachers, the government, our bosses. Just toss them out and let God tell us what to do? That would be fine if we really had a corner on God, and if he really always guided us by whispering commands in our ears. But he doesn't restrict himself to that; he uses human authority to guide us and, incidentally, to impose some order on this world.

Part of the reason many of us resent verses in the Bible that tell us to obey is that we think of authority strictly in terms of commands. Actually, that's just a small part of what the principle of authority is all about. You could think of a car's drive train as an example of authority. The clutch engages, one clutch plate responds to the authority of the other, and the result is that the car can go somewhere. It's really a way of working together; it's a sense of order.

Or think of ordering food in a restaurant. You could be as powerful as the President of the United States, yet you would still need to submit to the authority of the waitress. She tells you where to sit, she hands you the menu, she asks you what you'd like. If you got up out of your seat and tried to get your own meal, nothing would work correctly.

honor your uncle

I happen to believe that the family is a crucial area of society. If one family falls apart, the split is painful for the individuals but probably not for anyone else. But if half the families in a school neighborhood or in a country are falling apart, it's going to affect that school. It's going to affect that country. So when we're talking about the principle of authority, making things work together, one of the most crucial areas is right at home. "Honor your father and your mother," the Bible says.

Why should it work that way? Why not honor uncles or aunts? Why not have parents obey children? Well, I don't know precisely why. There may be a certain amount of arbitrariness to it; somebody had to be boss, and it came down to parents.

But in at least one sense it is not arbitrary. We know that in the Bible God is often referred to as "Father." There's deep wisdom in that. You can't see God, and it is hard to get a grip on what he is like. However, all of us know what fathers are like. Even if you have a poor father or even if your father is dead, you have some sense of the way an ideal father should be, and how you should relate to him. Fathers are living, breathing facts, and they are facts that God uses to teach us about himself. Specifically, as we learn to submit ourselves in love to our father's authority, not because we have to but because we want to, then we learn how to submit ourselves to God's authority. When you obey your parents you are learning about obeying (and loving) God. If you consistently refuse to honor your parents, it will be difficult to honor God.

Of course, there is a problem there—your parents aren't God. God won't ask you to do what isn't wise, but your parents might. So how do you deal with that?

When you're in the Army, they tell you something

salute the uniform

I believe is helpful. They say, "Don't salute the man, salute the uniform." Plenty of officers will rank above you who aren't worthy of the position they hold. They really aren't worthy of the respect symbolically represented in a salute. But the system has to be maintained. The system deserves respect, because it works. If every buck private could make up his own mind whom to salute and whom not to salute, the system would fall apart.

Today we're in a culture that has a lot of failure. The tendency is to add up all the failures and make the rules on the basis of them. There are so many bad marriages we want to throw away marriage as an institution. There are so many bad homes that we'll make new rules under which children run their own lives. There are so many bad schools that children won't have to obey; they can make all the rules themselves.

There's no question that authority gets abused. Some parents, for instance, are overstrict and rigid. But if those mistakes are allowed to define what parents are all about, and therefore parents stop trying to raise kids and let them raise themselves instead, I can promise you general chaos.

True, there are parents who don't deserve your respect. So what do you do? Run away from home? Resent and hate them? Revolt? Those are options, but they're options that place your individual happiness above everything else. Jesus offered a larger rule that takes in all those abuses and exceptions to the system. That's, "Love your enemies." If your father is a tyrant, how do you handle him? Try treating him with respect and love, by expecting proper guidance from him, by acting as though he were the kind of parent you wish he were. Salute the uniform, not the man; respect him as an individual. The surprising thing is that very often that kind of respect and love will bring out just the kind of behavior he should have had in the first place.

one man screamed

Our society does fall short of the ideal, and it's easy to accept and grow complacent about that, forgetting the ideal even exists. I remember taking a flight in a twin-engine airplane. In midair one engine quit. Even though the pilot warned us about it and assured us things would be all right, people panicked. One man stood up and cried and screamed. The stewardess was running and comforting people, trying to keep order. Every one of us felt fear in the pit of his stomach. But the plane just kept droning along, and after a while we realized that the pilot was right. We would make it safely. By the time we got to the end of the trip, we'd practically forgotten our fear. It seemed quite normal to be flying with only one engine.

Suddenly it dawned on me that we were getting used to something we had no business getting used to. The plane was badly damaged, but we'd practically forgotten that. It's the same in our society. Families are falling apart, but we change the rules and manage to limp along. Pretty soon we're all acting as though it's normal for half the families to fall apart. It isn't. One job Christians must do in our society is always point the direction back to the ideal that God intended for us. We do that partly by "saluting the uniform"—by recognizing that though, say, your parents aren't the best, respect and authority in a family are very, very important. It's the same thing in interacting with government, with churches, with teachers, with bosses, with anyone who is in authority over you (even waitresses). You respect the individual because you respect the system.

kings and soldiers

Of course, there are times to disobey. When my son was little we read the New Testament account of Herod killing the infants. My son asked, "Daddy, didn't the soldiers have babies of their own?"

"Yes," I said.

"Well, was the king bigger than the soldiers?"

"No. They were probably about the same size."

"Well, were there more kings than there were soldiers?"

"No, it was the other way around."

"Daddy," he said, "didn't they know that killing the babies was wrong?"

"Yes," I said, "they probably knew it. But when kings tell soldiers to do something, they do it."

He said, "Daddy, I don't care. If it was wrong, they shouldn't have done it."

This was the central issue behind the Nuremburg

trials, in which Nazis were tried for murder. Many of them pleaded innocent on the basis that they were commanded, on penalty of death, to kill helpless Jews. But for a Christian the issue is, whose authority is supreme? Ultimately, we serve Christ. We disobey whatever tells us to contradict his authority.

That rarely happens. I don't think there are very many times when our government or our parents or our schools tell us to do something contrary to what God wants us to do. But I do know that it happens. For 10 years now I've gotten letters from a girl whose father used to insist that she have sex with him three times a week. I told her not to do it. Eventually the situation became so severe that we had to put an ultimatum to him: either quit or we'd have him committed. He quit it, and she grew up, left home and now is happily married and has a family.

That's a rare situation, but it does happen. There are conflicts between the authority you find on earth and God's authority. "We must obey God rather than men."

two volumes of rules

Beyond that, keep in mind that authority is human. It's not a bunch of inflexible commands. You see that in the Bible. The Bible is not a book of ten thousand sins, but a book full of the experiences of men. Some of those lean in a God-ward way and some lean away from God. We read the long-range results of those leanings. We learn principles, not rules. If God's authority were reducible to a long list of dos and don'ts, then that's what God would have given us. If the laws of our land were reducible to a long list of commands, we wouldn't need judges and juries and presidents and congressmen and governors. We'd just have a couple of volumes called "The Rules." We don't have that. There are always gaps to laws, and that's why the legal libraries of our country are a lot bigger than "The Rules." They try to fill the gaps. But there's still always a need for individuals with wisdom to fill the gaps, and find the exceptions to the rules, and to apply the rules in a sensible way.

And the fact that authority is human means that it makes mistakes. The attitude it takes toward those mistakes makes a huge difference. I remember the contrast between the Kennedy administration and the Nixon administration when leaders spoke on college campuses. Kennedy would start off saying, "Look, I've made mistakes. Bay of Pigs was a terrible mistake which we're still paying for. Now I want to admit that and tell you where I think we can go from here."

The Nixon administration was different. Its leaders tended to be defensive; they drew hostility like honey draws flies. Instead of admitting mistakes, they'd try to ignore them. "Why do you want to look at the hole instead of the doughnut?" they'd say. "Look at all the good things we've done." But their attitude of defensiveness eroded rather than strengthened their authority. Any authority figure who can face his mistakes openly has gained, not lost.

If you want to help the authorities in your life be more worthy of respect, figure out ways to get them off the defensive. Treat them with respect and honor and let them know you don't respect them less because they make mistakes. Let them know they can be open about their own failures by being open about your own. Try it with your parents, your teachers, your boss. Over a period of time it will make a difference.

the principle of order

Authority is the principle by which order is maintained, the principle which lets people work together. We live in a mixed universe, wherein sin has put people in rebellion against authority, and authority itself is sometimes badly corrupted. But we must not, as Christians, make the mistake of giving up on authority, or of giving up on the ways of working together God has given us.

Families are important; therefore, obey your parents. Learning from older, wiser people is important; therefore, respect your teachers. We need government; therefore, respect the law and the people who carry it out. The reward that will come if this is done in love is a deeper respect for the God who made all these things, and a deeper harmony in the world you live in.

what good is church?

Why not start your own church?
A church that's young, spontaneous, free. . . .

It's happened a number of times in the last few years. A young person in high school or college has approached me about starting a Bible study at our house. "Hey, Jay, do you think we could use your home?"

I'll say, "When did you have in mind?" and he'll say, a lot of the time, "How about Sunday?" As we talk, I find out that what he really has in mind is starting a substitute for church, a kind of youth church. Of course, none of them plans on excluding anyone else, but when you dig under the surface, each one wants a group that is composed of people like him: same age, same interests, same problems, same political views.

When you go beyond that and question what they're doing, you find that they're basically unhappy with the established churches. Often it's the politics that bugs them; the churches they've attended seem to think that conservatism in politics and theology go hand in hand, and they don't buy that. They and most of their friends believe in pacifism, civil rights and other causes, and the church doesn't.

Or it may be the style of worship they don't like. They feel they should be accepted in blue jeans, and the church favors dresses and coats and ties. They want to be spontaneous, and the church has an established order of worship. They want to sing with guitars, and the church likes organs. They don't fit in, they don't feel they're being listened to, and consequently they want to start a group of people like them.

Not that most young people want to start their

own church. Most kids I've met aren't troubled about church. It's not a gut-level issue with them, for one of two reasons: either they don't go, or they turn it off. They form a mutual nonaggression pact with their parents. I had this sort of thing when I was young. Mom would say, "You can stay up all hours on Saturday night, but you've got to get up and go to church on Sunday morning." It didn't matter what I got out of church, if I could get my body into a vertical position in church Sunday morning, I'd met the conditions. The same with a lot of churchgoers. They've bought peace at home. It's a small payment, really—two hours on Sunday to get your parents off your back for the rest of the week.

the Lone Ranger

Of these two groups—those who want to form their own "youth" church, and those who sit in church wondering who's winning between the Vikings and the Patriots—I'd have to say I'm closer to the first. At least they care. At least they look at church and expect something from it.

I will never make it as a Christian alone. In fact, there is no such thing as a Christian completely alone. A built-in part of Christianity is being in fellowship, gathering to worship God with people who believe in him.

Of course, what the Bible calls "the church" isn't a building, or a set of doctrinal beliefs, or something officially announced in the bulletin. The church is the believers in Christ, throughout the world, and specifically, the church is the believers who gather in each area—each town, each neighborhood. They may gather in a house, they may meet in the woods, they may meet in a cathedral—they're still the church. So the fact that the "youth" church wants to meet in my living room doesn't bother me. What bothers me is that it's an attempt to get away from problems that, sooner or later, must be faced.

You see, I've watched a number of these small groups progress. Interestingly enough, the members don't stay young. They tend to get older year by year. Pretty soon some of them marry and have kids. Well, then John and Mary can't come, because their baby is crying all the time. Ted and Alicia have a baby, and the same problem comes up. The rest of the group doesn't like not seeing those four, so they finally discuss getting a sitter. Eventually they get volunteers to take care of the children at different meetings.

When their kids get older, they begin to wonder if having them play with Tinker Toys all the time is the best option. "Maybe we should try to teach them about Jesus?" So they try teaching them in various ways, and they stumble over a technique that holds their attention pretty well: flannelgraphs. Pretty soon you have a whole Sunday school set up.

Then there's the building. At some point it usually gets pretty crowded in the living room you're meeting in. The furniture gets scratched. Sometimes the people who own the house are out of town, and that makes complications. So, you rent a hall somewhere. But there are always conflicts with that, too: other people want to use the building at the same time, and the rent gets expensive, and the facilities aren't quite right. Ninety percent of these groups build a church building within about twenty years. Other changes come. Soon you have a group that's evolved into something that looks a lot like what we call the establishment church, except that it took twenty years to get there.

homogenized?

I have a couple of problems with that process. First of all, why put all that time and energy into something that ends up looking like what you set out to escape? If that's the result, why not work on changing the bad things instead of starting over? In twenty years you might end up with some changes that are pretty good. That makes a twenty-year head start on the "youth" church.

The other problem is tied up with the whole question of what the church is, and what it's meant to be. Is the church meant to be perfect, constantly enjoyable, never grating? I don't believe so.

In my view, the church is not a homogenous group. People don't and shouldn't have all the same age, the same political views, the same income, the same skin color, the same politics or the same basic approach to life.

I see the church's job as being something like making ball bearings. To make ball bearings, you get a whole bunch of fairly rough pieces of metal, and you put them in a centerless grinder. Then you get an abrasive like diamond dust or carborundum, and you add it along with a lot of oil. You spin the whole thing with tremendous speed, and the oil moves things around while the metal grates against metal and abrasive. You end up with those imperfect little pieces of metal ground into bright, perfect little ball bearings.

The church is the same way. You take the young and the old, the wise and the ignorant, and you give them real life experiences. They can't just sit around in an ivory tower talking about Bible verses in a theoretical way. That wouldn't do any good. But if you deal with the real implications of Christ's life in things like family, sex, jobs, worship and money, you are going to wear on each other. The love of God is the oil—it makes it possible for the surfaces to wear on each other without burning each other up. Everything spins around, and we're able to rub the rough edges off one another.

I may have a particular political view, but in trying to understand the other guy in a loving way, I find that he has something to say. I develop tolerance and patience, things that God really likes to see, if I'm the impatient type. If I'm the complacent type, the impatient people tend to stir me up. All together we mix and wear on each other so we can become a community. In a way, it's the imperfections in the church that make it useful. If we're all the same, we may agree and have a good time, but we never grow.

how long is a foot?

If that's what the church is meant to be, then it makes sense that there ought to be all kinds of people in it—the more kinds the better—so as to balance each other. Unfortunately, our society isn't constructed that way, and so neither are churches, because churches aren't synonymous with the kingdom of God. They tend to reflect society at large. Our society tends to be divided along racial lines; so are churches. Our society tends to separate the upper classes from the lower classes. So do churches. And, of course, there are national and geographic boundaries, so that we in America lose the balancing, shaping influence of, say, African Christians. Our ball bearings tend to develop bulges on one side, because they have an out-of-balance perspective. If everyone in your church is from a rich background, everyone tends to have a rich man's point of view, a view not necessarily in line with the truth. The same is true of a group of believers in a poor neighborhood.

Is everything about the shaping process relative? Does it just depend on the background of the people in the church? It often does, sadly. But it doesn't have to. Two factors can change that. The first is recognizing the outside factors that have determined how you think. Your feelings and ideas do tend to be a creation of your background. If you like having a good car, it's a bet your parents do, too. If classical music isn't your thing, it probably isn't your parents', either. Once you realize that a lot of outside factors influenced your ideas, you become more open to change.

More important, I think, is the fact that we have a standard to bring our ideas up against. That standard is the word of God—the Bible. Everyone, no matter how much he's broadened his base of experience, still has ideas that are a result of his own relative experience.

But you go to church not to be led by a man, but to be led by Christ. At the Bureau of Standards they have measurements that are the ultimate standards. How do you know exactly how long a foot is? Every yardstick is off a little, because there's human and machine error in it. But if you want to know how long a foot is, they have a ruler at the Bureau of Standards that is exactly a foot. Nobody, no matter how powerful he or she is, can argue with that ultimate standard. No one can change it.

When we come before the Word of God, it's like that. All of us are equal before God—the smart and the slow, the wise and the foolish, the rich and the poor. At church, the idea is to bring our relativistic ideas and measure them against the Word of God. The Holy Spirit works in our lives to help us understand that measure. We adjust our ideas and our lives accordingly, and are brought to a basis of agreement. It doesn't mean we won't differ. God's intention isn't to make us exactly identical. But we do have a standard to bring our own ideas before—something that corrects us, and tells us when we're really out of whack.

revolution

But not everyone in your church is likely to see things in those idealistic terms. It's sad, but there are few older people who listen to young people with the idea of growing through what's being said. They want them to conform, to "straighten up."

I said before that the church isn't synonymous with the kingdom of God. It's partly a human institution, fallible just as everything else is in our world. It tends to be a microcosm of society in general. That's why it doesn't surprise me a great deal to know that young people have a hard time adjusting and fitting into the church. They have a hard time adjusting and fitting into society in general.

But assuming that you believe what the Bible says, that the church is the place where we're supposed to grow as believers in Christ, then it seems to me there are three possible ways to approach it, just as there are only a few ways to approach changing society.

The first option is the revolutionary one. You tear down or bypass the system and build another. The only trouble is, you find most revolutionaries end up looking just like what they were revolting against. That's what happens in the "youth" church we were discussing before—you go off and start over, but you end up exactly where you started.

Another option is to get inside the structure of the system and try to change it from within. You play the game, in other words, and gain enough power and influence to have things your own way. The only trouble is that before long you've adopted the same characteristics you wanted to change. You've been eaten up by the system. "We have met the enemy and he is us," in the immortal words of Pogo.

But there is a third option, what I call modeling. I believe it's what Jesus did. Jesus really wasn't much of a revolutionary, despite what some say. He did not take on the system to radically change it, at least not in the usual "revolutionary" way. On the other hand, he wasn't much of a joiner. He didn't go study and work his way up to being chief priest, then gradually bring in reforms. No, what Jesus did was act as a living example of another way. He represented the kingdom of God, and people who observed him were struck with another alternative in life.

In a smaller way, this is what you should do when you go to church. If you believe you have a greater capacity for tolerance, love and understanding than your bigoted, conservative elders, show it by being more tolerant. Show it by sitting and listening for long periods of time, by waiting, by turning the other cheek, by being a model of what a Christian is. When you turn the other cheek, you're giving the intolerant man the chance to see a new way of acting. You've unsettled him. Maybe he never lets you know that. Maybe it takes a long time before he realizes, "You know, that young man acts different. . . ." Does it matter? This is the way to make a difference in a loving way, and to bring about changes that come from the heart—changes that are really changes, not just changes on the surface.

don't sit in a corner

I'm not suggesting you go sit in a corner and think nice thoughts, hoping someone will decide to change things. You have to be willing to confront people lovingly on certain issues. You must be willing to ask questions like, "Why do we do it that way?" This can be a great gift young people bring to a church, because every church needs to re-evaluate.

I am suggesting that two factors are critical in the way you question. The first is that your questions come, not from simply wanting your own way, but from really caring about the people in that church. If you walk in, and on the first Sunday you want to turn the whole church upside down, people aren't going to think much of it. You may have to wait patiently a few years before people really know that you are committed to them. Your love for people in your church has to be unconditional, not, "If you don't do things my way, I'm leaving."

Second, you have to realize that one man's meat is another man's poison. We all have some basic needs that are the same, but those needs are filled in a lot of different ways. A guitar may be the very best thing for your kind of singing, but if someone else likes hearing Bach, you can't say, "That's junk." A person who's eighteen probably has slightly different needs from a person who's sixty. When you ask questions and honestly, openly listen to the answers, you discover that. Young people tend to be less conservative because they have less to conserve. Older people don't usually want to spend all their time going from one little meeting to the next because they have families and jobs that are taking up a great deal of their time. There are good reasons for people feeling the way they do, at least part of the time. Developing tolerance and patience with each other is part of what's exciting about the body of Christ.

Frankly, the church is the only institution in our society which has a chance to do this. That's one reason I'm probably more excited about church than anything else in my life today. Every other group is tied to productivity in some way, and those who seemingly can't keep pace and contribute get shunted aside. The old get put in homes. The young aren't listened to. Women get shoved aside. If you can "produce," you're valuable, and your opinions are listened to. Otherwise, forget it.

But the church, the body of Christ, can be different. There's no product involved. Nobody has to be able to work so many hours, put out so much "product." It's one place where the old are valuable, where the young are valuable—just as valuable as anyone else. In the church you can form a community with people truly different from yourself. That's one of the church's most precious gifts. It's the differences in a church that make it valuable. Sameness wouldn't expand your horizons or make you truly grow.

But it has to start with you. The dog-eat-dog attitude of the world shouldn't exist in the body of Christ. We are to have an attitude of love. We are governed by the ground rules of the New Testament, the basic rule of which is, "love your neighbor as yourself." That opens us to genuine security with each other. There's potential for really baring our problems, so that others can help us bear them.

So I'd say this: allow yourself to be frustrated with church. The only way to avoid frustration is to expect nothing. The church has such great potential, we need to expect a lot. Otherwise we won't reach our potential.

But however frustrated you get, stay with it. Don't cop out by sitting like a mannequin propped up in your pew, not caring a bit. Don't stop going. Don't try to run from the differences of opinion you find. Face them. Face the problems. And begin to discover the joy that comes with being molded into what God wants you to be. He does it through his body, the church.

why work?

Who wants to work when you could be flying high?

We got a letter the other day, typed on plain white paper, with quite a few mistakes. The paper had been folded about eight times to fit the envelope. It was from a girl in New York.

She said, "I really love what you're doing. You've helped me so much by dealing with those touchy everyday problems. But there is one area which, so far as I know, you haven't hit. I'm sure that every kid has hassles with it as much as I do. I hate it. The subject is work."

From the buildup, I'd been expecting maybe abortion, violence in school, or parents. But work? If you're still in school, you only work in the off-hours. Is work a major issue?

In a way, it has to be. After all, what will you be doing the rest of your life? Not taking tests, skiing or making love. You'll spend thousands and thousands of hours working. If you're unhappy with work, you'll be a very unhappy person.

But when I think about work, I don't get unpleasant thoughts. I've done practically every kind of job at some point in my life; I've dug ditches and baled hay, and I've also been the president of Youth For Christ, International and spoken to crowds of thousands. No job really stands out in my mind as an unhappy experience. In fact, when I think of the difference between baling hay and being president of a large organization, the similarities jump out before the differences. Every job I've ever had involves both pain and pleasure, and which one dominates seems to depend more on me than on the job.

From a purely aesthetic point of view, the best

job I ever had was working as a draftsman for the Indiana Tollway. I've never felt more like Michelangelo. I loved working with the pens, the different colors of ink on fine linen, the exacting process of putting each line down perfectly, with the right weight, color and dimension.

That job could be, very literally, a pain. Often we had to work overtime, sometimes twelve hours straight bending over a drafting board. It was physically tough. It was hard on your eyes, excruciatingly painful for your back. But I still enjoyed it. I always figured that any job had its trade-off of pain and pleasure.

beyond the paycheck

Evidently, some things have changed. I don't think I'm exceptional in enjoying most jobs; I grew up in an environment where people expected different things from a job than most people do today. What's changed?

Most Americans used to work to survive. They didn't work for creativity or wholeness; they worked to fill the emptiness in their stomach. There are still people in America who work for that reason, and many others are forced to work to keep up with the cars and boats and houses they've bought. But if you work, it's probably for something you could do without—better clothes, or a car. Since you are not worrying about survival, you expect other things from a job. You start looking beyond the paycheck and think how the time spent working compares with, say, painting a picture or water-skiing. These kind of comparisons never occurred to people a few years ago.

There's also a greater awareness today. I used to think that, basically, you got paid what the job was worth. If you worked harder, you would earn more.

I now realize that's not the way capitalism works. Theoretically, the amount you get paid is based on how scarce your kind of labor is, or how hard you would be to replace. It's often the hardest jobs which get paid least. Look at a construction crew sometime. The harder they work, the less the pay. The concrete guys sweat the most and get the least. The finishing carpenter gets paid more than the framing carpenter, even though he doesn't have to wrestle two-by-fours around. Why? His skills are harder to replace. When you think beyond that to other classes of labor—the people who manage, and those who put up the money to get things going—you're talking about even more pay.

Naturally, if you realize that, your first reaction is, "What am I doing turning hamburgers? The real money is in sitting back and watching the customers come in, like the owner does." You realize you can't afford to purchase your own hamburger stand, but you resent the guy who can. You notice that when a financial crunch comes, the workers are first to be laid off, not the owners and the managers. You can easily begin to feel as though you're being used, like a draft animal.

Besides that, the whole work ethic is being challenged. When I was a kid it was assumed that work was good. The harder the worker the better the person. But now that's in question. People travel, and they notice other countries don't necessarily feel the same way about work. In France they shut down the whole country for the month of August— the factories, most of the stores, the repair shops, everything closes. Vacations are more important to people there. You look at the Bible. How important was work to them? We know that the disciples were willing to leave their jobs to follow Jesus for three years. Can you imagine what people would say about that today? It wouldn't be thought very responsible.

assembly-line specialists

Notice one thing about all these factors: they're attitudes. Some say people are unhappy about their jobs because the work has changed. They say the assembly line and the slap-it-together philosophy have ruined any sense of craftsmanship, have dehumanized workers and made them feel like machines. Probably there's some truth to it, but I personally think it's vastly overestimated. I grew up with lower-class working people, and I know that there can be pride and skill in just about any job you name, including assembly-line positions. An assembly line can nearly kill a new guy; I've had people tell me they had nightmares about being buried under the stream of cars or radios coming at them. But an assembly-line worker is essentially a specialist—he knows he can do his own job better than anyone else and if he's smart he takes pride in the way he does it.

I've known men who took great pride in the particular weld they made on each car. There are some signs that kind of pride is on the increase. I think it's wonderful that some young people are opting for jobs that let them get their hands on what's being produced instead of just thinking about it. Kids with college or even graduate degrees are choosing to be carpenters, farmers, shepherds.

I read in the **New Yorker** recently about a couple who had gone back to an ethnic neighborhood in New York and bought a corner grocery, not for the money but so they could be in touch with the people there. Some of these trends are just nostalgia, and they'll last about as long as the money from home does. But some are for real. I hope it extends itself into other areas. There is room for real pride and fulfillment managing an office, or organizing a whole series of little jobs so that everything gets done. There's room for pride in typing.

It's encouraging that some people are seeing you don't have to be a doctor or a lawyer to be worthwhile. There is just as much dignity in plumbing as being a lawyer. If you don't think so, see how long it takes a lawyer to do a plumbing job that would take a professional about thirty minutes.

down to earth

Let's get down to earth and talk about what this has to do with working a part-time or summer job. There, your choices are limited. You aren't going to get the jobs everybody else wants—you're lucky if you get any job at all.

Still, you ought to think about what you want to gain before you start working. You ought to look for the rewards and pains in a job. And those "rewards" shouldn't be seen simply in terms of whether it's a fun job. The paycheck is one important reward. If you're working just because you don't have anything else to do, why don't you volunteer in a nursing home, or work in politics? You'll probably experience things you'll never forget, which may not be the case at Burger King.

But most people who work have something in mind, like saving for college or taking a trip. Before you start a job, take out a pencil and write down what you intend to do with the money. If they're things that really aren't important, forget the job. If they are, then stick to the job.

There's another aspect of long-term rewards: learning about yourself. As I said earlier, working is how you'll spend a lot of your life. Some of the less pleasant jobs can give you insight into what kind of work you like. Do you like being inside using your head, or outside using your muscles? Do you like being your own boss, or do you prefer having someone else give you directions? Do you enjoy working with people or numbers? A lot of people get out of school without the foggiest idea how to answer those questions.

Just sweeping up in a stockbroker's office will give you some ideas about the kind of life the stockbroker has. Before you look for a job, think about what you want to learn. Don't always take the first job that's offered you. Go looking and asking. Explain what you're interested in learning. Believe me, an employer is impressed by someone who has an interest that goes beyond the paycheck.

search for pleasure

Once you're in a job, make up your mind to enjoy it. That makes so much difference, it's a wonder more people don't try it. You can control your attitude, and when your attitude is right your feelings come around.

Take me, for instance. Occasionally I have to go home after a long day at work and dig a ditch to put some plumbing in. I don't think anyone thinks of digging ditches as the most pleasant job in the world. But I try to think about it in advance. I think about the pleasures of working outside where I can feel the sun, look at the sky and sometimes hear the birds sing. I think about the pleasure of working with my body and feeling the sweat roll down my arms. I think of how wonderful it is to quit a job knowing that something tangible has been accomplished: a ditch is dug, and that particular ditch will never need to be dug again.

Rewards can be found in any job, and if you look for them, you'll find them.

Here are five things I'd suggest you look for.

1. Look for pride. Maybe you're not getting paid so much as the boss, but there are certain things you're doing that he isn't. Take a group of carpenters and let them listen to a developer showing off some houses. The developer says, "I built that house, and that one, and that one." Inside every

carpenter is the same thought. "You never build anything. You probably can't hammer a nail straight." What the developer means is that he arranged the financing, bought the property, called the union and hired the carpenters. But he didn't build the house. Only the carpenter can say that. He's got a good sense of pride.

That same sense comes in any number of jobs. "I cleaned that office and man, it shines. I fed a thousand people today, right off my grill." If what you're involved in isn't worth doing, don't do it. Quit. I wouldn't encourage you to sell your soul just to get a paycheck. But the truth is, most jobs aren't like that. In some way they contribute something that has to be done, and done well. You should take pride in that.

2. Look for growth. Brother Lawrence, who wrote **Practicing His Presence,** has been revered by millions for what he learned as the scullery cook in a monastery. He tried to be actively aware of God while he worked. In doing so he developed a character that drew spiritually hungry people to him.

A waitress has lots of chances to learn patience and cheerfulness. A worker in a noisy factory has time to think and pray and memorize Scripture. Think about how you want to grow, and look for opportunities in your job. Don't let your mind vegetate.

3. Look for people. One great thing about work is that you meet people you'd never encounter in school. Sometimes that's pleasant, and sometimes it's a shock. Either way, you can learn.

One of the greatest lessons I ever learned about love was from a guy from Notre Dame. We worked one summer loading trucks, and I looked up to him tremendously. We'd eat lunch together, and when girls came into the restaurant, guys would make comments about them. But this guy always seemed to be incredibly in love with his wife. One time I got up the courage to ask him, "Man, don't you ever look at other women?"

"Oh, yeah," he said, "lots of times. But I figure I'll always find a girl who has a better body or mind or prettier hair than my wife. But I didn't marry a body or a mind or hair. I married a total person. A woman is more than one thing."

I was in high school, and that was the first time something like that had ever occurred to me. It impressed me a lot.

I've also worked with guys from whom I learned negative lessons. I remember one guy who was a genius with wood. He could work miracles to make beautiful grain and texture come out. But he was a drunk, a wino. One day he came to work and had a spasm, and fell down on the floor. He'd died. I had to call the police and get them to come to get him. Believe me, I remembered.

4. Look for ministry. Generally your boss is not paying you to counsel and spend your time in conversation with others. If you're being paid to work, it's wrong to do anything else. But there are ways and times to reach out to people, and there are people who are affected just by the fact that you're consistent and honest, even if they don't show it. As-

sume that the people you work with, even the bosses, are somewhat unsure of themselves and afraid. Assume that God has put you in your job to be available to those people, and I think you'll be used in some way. Even a smile can help someone else.

5. Look for a chance to express yourself. This is the toughest assignment, and it requires creativity. In one factory I heard of, they encouraged the workers to paint their own machines. Some of them paint them in bright colors, others make them look like huge animals. I think it's a great idea, and I'll bet the workers have a lot of fun at it.

If you're happy, and the job allows it, whistle a tune. Decorate your space or your uniform. Do your work with a special flourish. Let yourself enjoy what you're doing.

a quarter-inch of dirt

Work isn't all pleasure, as you know. There is pain, and you can't ignore it. Instead, you should look for the rewards and consider them a trade-off for the pain you go through. Look at the job as a whole and don't let the bad things get on your nerves.

Baling hay is one of the toughest physical jobs there is. You can literally have dirt covering your body a quarter-inch thick. You breathe in the hay and choke. Bugs crawl all over you. You get so exhausted you think you're going to expire. You're sure you'll never lift another hay bale over your head.

But there are also rewards. The cleaning up afterwards, the wrestling at lunch hour, the barn full of hay, the sweat dripping off your nose, lifting something another person couldn't, being scared you couldn't keep up all day and finding out some guy bigger than you sat down before you did . . . plus the paycheck . . . those are the rewards. You find out that, if your attitude's right, it will more than balance out the pain.

A basic part of the right attitude is knowing whom you're working for. A Christian is never working for a company or an employer. He's working for God. If you start worrying about all the internal hassles of the place where you're working, it'll ruin your attitude. Is this person doing his share? Is that person being unfairly favored? You don't have to borrow those troubles if you're working for God. Nor do you try to get away with things. Sometimes people goof off on a job because no one's watching. Ironically, they cheat themselves as much as the boss. Not only do they lose self-respect, because they have no pride in what they're doing, but they also make the day twice as long. There's nothing worse than a job where you have to sit around twiddling your thumbs.

But if you're working for God, you're not tempted to goof off. You're not affected by other people's attitudes and problems. You're there for God, and no number of problems is going to change that.

When you do run into hassles, remember your original decision. You chose to work there; no one coerced you. You knew, if you had any sense at all, that there would be pain as well as pleasure in the job. But you looked at the long-term goals, and you decided it was worth it for the money and the experience.

Don't ever be ashamed to take your paycheck. My dad used to tell me, "Don't ever back up to the pay window." You do your work right, and you earn the pay. It's yours—the boss isn't doing you a big favor. That's his side of the agreement. Yours is to work. If you realize that the job isn't what you thought it would be, or if you've come to the point where you want to try something else, then find another job. There's no reason to stay at one job, especially when you're just trying things out. Just make sure you're leaving the job behind, and not trying to run away from your own bad attitudes.

But if you stay, don't gripe. Don't develop a bad attitude. Don't let the pain overwhelm the pleasures. Look for the rewards. There are sure to be some.

I was brought up to believe that work, any work, is good. Like the guy whose mother always told him, "Take out the garbage; it'll build your character."

I'd have to modify that now. I don't think work itself is good. You can work to do something good or you can work to do something bad. You can work in a way that's healthy and satisfying, or you can destroy yourself with complaining. Work is really neutral, neither good nor bad. You're going to do a lot of it in life, and all of it will have one basic characteristic: there will be both pain and pleasure. Now's the time to find the pleasure and fulfillment. The pattern can last a long time.

who cares

about Bangladesh?

Photo: Ed Wallowitch

**Babies starving in Bangladesh?
What's it to me?**

In India I began to understand how deep the problems of poor people go. I was walking down a street with a friend when I heard an odd noise behind me. There was a click followed by a swishing sound, then another click and a swish, and more. I turned around to see what it was. I saw a little boy, perhaps twelve years old, whose legs were gone. He had two short, hand-made crutches about 18 inches long with which he pulled himself along the streets. That made the sound—click when he put down the crutches, swish when he dragged his body over the streets.

He asked me for money. What could I do? I was moved by his situation. I reached into my pocket where I'd collected a number of Indian coins, and I emptied a handful into his hands. I didn't think about the fact that I was probably giving him more than a grown man there earned in several days; I just gave him the coins.

Almost immediately there was a reaction. From doorways and alleys people spilled out, more than I could believe. They attacked the boy, hitting him and jumping on him, taking his money away. I tried to help him, shoving them away while he held onto the money for dear life. But they got most of it. He crawled over to the side of the street with perhaps one or two of the coins left. Strangely, though, he didn't seem very unhappy about the whole affair.

That's a world no person who lives in America can really understand or judge. Naturally, I was upset at the greed that could steal so brazenly from the boy. But what did I know about the kind of life that exists day after day with the serious possibility of starving to death?

But though that world of hunger and poverty is one I can't fully understand, I can't afford to ignore it. Not any longer! The world is changing, and the hungry nations aren't just sitting by passively hoping for a handout. They are becoming more and more outspoken in their demands. They are questioning whether we have any rights to our riches. Americans are beginning to hear the sounds of the masses just as in the medieval days when men defended castles. Knights then would be trapped inside, looking out through slits in the walls, listening to the pounding of their enemies at the door or the digging at the base of the castle where their enemies tried to make the walls collapse. Today, the rich Western peoples are surrounded by a massive nuclear moat, hoping it will hold off the hungry people outside. Increasingly we hear the pounding at the door.

baby at the door

Increased population is responsible for many of the problems, but I don't think that's the whole story. People have been starving and dying of diseases all through history. The real change is the shrinking of the globe—the increased communications. We are aware of people we had never heard of before.

I think any Christian person would respond with love and care to a baby left on his doorstep. If the baby were starving, he would feed it. If the baby were on the road in front of his house, he would still feel a compulsion to go out and feed it. Even put the baby clear down on the end of the block, and he would probably walk clear to the end of the block to feed it. However, if you move that baby to India, he probably won't feel the same responsibility. But the moral problem is no different. A baby starving in India or Africa is no different from a baby starving on our doorstep. And in a sense, with the growth of communication systems like radio and television, the world has become our doorstep. We know about those starving babies; we even see them on TV. And how can we ignore them, let alone ignore the poor and starving of our own country?

That is why I've personally agonized over this question of wealth as much as any other single thing. We have got to evaluate our life-style and begin asking ourselves on a personal basis, "Is there a line of richness beyond which I cannot go? Am I really dealing with my responsibility to give time and money to others? Do I really love, or do I only love those people when it's painless?" We are the richest people in the history of the world. It only makes sense that our greatest temptations should come in the area of wealth.

the one-camel family

The Bible doesn't raise this question in quite the way it's raised today. Its first concern in the matter of wealth isn't whether a Christian ought to own one camel or two. It talks first of all about the philosophy of materialism—the "ism" that says the world is simply material, and that's all there is to it. The answer to any problem, according to this philosophy, lies in material, and that's why a genuine materialist puts his faith in material goods. I believe that's wnat Jesus is attacking in Matthew 6 when he says, "Don't store up treasures here on earth where they can erode away or may be stolen. Store them in heaven where they . . . are safe from thieves." He talked about the transitory nature of things—that someday this very planet will be used up, finished—but said there are living, eternal qualities, spiritual things, that will go on forever. In 1 Corinthians 13 Paul talks about the things that won't last, and he even includes things like knowledge and the ability to communicate. The only things that will last, he concludes, are faith, hope and love —spiritual qualities with eternal significance. The person who thinks "things" are the key to life is on the wrong track.

But there is also a second concern you find in the Bible: I recently heard Richard Halverson, pastor of Fourth Presbyterian Church in Washington, D.C., speak about this. He said he had taken out a concordance and done an exhaustive study of what the Bible has to say about wealth and about the poor. One thing stood out to him. He said he found that unrighteousness and neglect of the poor are virtually synonymous in the Bible. When the Bible talks about the kind of life that God loves to see, it virtually always includes something about caring for oppressed and poor people. When Israel was in trouble in the Old Testament, she would often accelerate her worship, her Bible reading and prayer. But that wasn't what God was looking to see. He saw that the neglect of the poor continued, and he would judge and condemn her.

I concur fully with Halverson's feelings. If we're to look honestly at what Scripture says, we have to conclude that the way we deal with the poor is integrally tied with a healthy response to God.

Of course, you meet a lot of people who are very concerned about the poor, but often it seems to be all talk. Their sacrifices are minimal. They don't give up money or time when it really hurts. Some people who talk well can't even find time for the needs of the people next door. Or they may find money to give to the poor, but they don't have any time to give. Most of the poor I know would prefer that you befriend them and care for them as people rather than that you drop off some money. There is a world of difference between the person who is philosophically committed to dealing with the problems of poverty and the person who has really made himself vulnerable by acting on his beliefs. This is what God wants.

But with real commitment problems come. The situation is very much more complex than it seems at first. Like my experience in India—I thought I was doing something kind in giving money to the beggar boy. However, human greed destroyed most of the good I'd intended for him. The same is true of other things on a much larger scale. With the increase in population, there is the really serious question whether **any** amount of giveaways would forestall starvation. Perhaps it even eventually makes things worse, by allowing people to survive now and starve in greater numbers later. And then there are the factors of bureaucracy and greed. Suppose I gave my dollar to a volunteer agency. Suppose I decided not to eat hamburgers at Burger King because beef is a very inefficient producer of protein. How is that really going to affect the baby in Bangladesh? Will my dollar be eaten up by politicians or by greedy merchants? Even if it gets there, will it be a drop in the bucket, a meaningless crumb in the face of a problem that is bigger than I am, perhaps bigger than the resources of the entire world?

sell all and give to the poor

What can I do that will make a difference? Should I give up all my money and live in total, abject poverty? There was a point in my life where I tried that. My wife Janie and I had almost nothing—we gave it all away. For years I lived in basements and attics. I gave that lifestyle up because I couldn't see how it was doing anyone any good. I'd given up so much I'd disqualified myself from helping anyone. I didn't even have the gas to get out of my yard to go help someone. I had given everything away.

At another point, later on, I had the desire to move into a ghetto in Chicago to see if I could pick up cans and bottles from my yard as quickly as people could throw them there. But as I thought about that, I realized I'd be putting pressure on my wife and kids rather than on myself. And would it really solve anything? And if I were to sell all and give to the poor, then how poor would I want to become? Do I want to identify with the poor of a Chicago ghetto? By certain African or Indian standards, American poverty is gaudily rich. Do I go all the way and starve to death, identifying with the poor of Bangladesh? If so, what good have I done? These are the agonized questions I've asked myself time and again.

I don't think I've come up with any final answer, and so far as I can see no one else has either. I am fairly sure that there is no absolute answer for everyone; that what is right for one person may not be right for someone else. And I am also fairly sure that giving everything away and joining the counterculture is not the answer to the problems of poverty. I don't help anyone by buying a pair of $12.96 genuine Levis and living from hand to mouth, maybe even begging from people on the street and then criticizing them for their lifestyle. I don't help anyone by living off the land in a commune or living off a compassionate father who sends me money. I have concluded that there are real advantages to the kind of life that punches a clock and earns a living producing something worthwhile.

So what do I do, beyond earning a living and maybe sending off a check to Compassion or World Vision? That brings in institutions. I once felt you could change the world just by changing individuals. I'd go beyond that now: I'm more and more convinced that the world is changed when you change individuals who commit themselves to changing institutions, which then change the world. Government in particular is going to be, in our age, the primary agency through which the starving are fed or not fed.

I hope that when I hear politicians talking about "rugged individualism" and "America first" that I will react immediately by saying, "This is not a Christian way of looking at life." God says we should love our brothers, and I am committed to doing that politically as well as personally.

they die one at a time

At the same time, I know government will never solve a problem people aren't willing to combat themselves, individually. I know that there is really no such thing as reducing the percentage of unemployment. You are either employed or you are unemployed—helping unemployed people happens one person at a time. No one ever increased his employment three percent just because the government statistics said it happened. The same with starving people—you either have enough food or you don't. People die one at a time. Even if one person can't help everybody, all help must begin with a single individual and a single act. If I can't offer money I can offer dignity. If I can't offer food I can offer time.

And of course, one of the positive things about the free-enterprise system is that I can go out, starting with a little money, and generate a large amount of money if I'm successful. It may be that's the role some of us should play. After all, someone had to start Ford Motor Company—why not have it be someone who's committed to using the profits to feed hungry people rather than to buy yachts? There is a place for individual initiative, whether it's developing a business whose profits might help poor people, or whether it's moving into the ghetto to work on a project of immediate significance in helping people.

Personally, I know God hasn't called me to do either of those things. The chief thrust of my life is to work on the task of leading people to Jesus Christ. And most of us simply aren't going to be called into the ghetto, or into politics, or into big finance. Most of us are going to be accountants and carpenters and secretaries and teachers—jobs where we have limited amounts of money and limited amounts of influence.

But there are things that we can do. For one thing, we can be sensitive to the problem politically. We can also give what we're able to give. And that raises the issue of how we live. We have, in my family, tried to stress two principles: "make do" and "simplify." When we want to replace something, we really ask hard, "Can we 'make do' with what we have? Can it last another year? Or can we find some ways to fix up the old thing so that it works well?"

And then we look for ways to simplify. This isn't just in the interests of saving money. It's in the interests of our own sanity. I've found that many so-called "labor-saving devices" are actually terribly consuming. You have to keep fixing them when they break down. You constantly put them away and take them out again. Gadgets complicate your life, they don't simplify it.

poor materialists

The question to me is, what dollars can I free productively to do what God wants? There are those who think that money itself is the big evil—that you have to get rid of it so it won't soil you or seduce you into sin. I don't think they know what they are talking about. I've been poor most of my life, grew up poor and lived around relatively poor people. I know I've met just as many materialists among the poor as among the rich. It's very tempting to care about nothing but money when you're poor. It's easy to think that if you just had enough money all your problems would be solved. But of course, that is a total illusion, and I think I've met more people among the sons and daughters of rich people who knew how much it was an illusion. They have drunk from the wells of money and have found the water acrid. It doesn't satisfy. Many, out of laziness and habit, may continue to live the same life. But many others become very aware of the spiritual dimensions of life and of their responsibility to use money wisely. That may take a different form from what you'd expect. They may not give it all away and go live in a shack. Instead, they may be plowing it back into the business. But is it just greed making them do that? Not always.

I know a man who is the head of a very large company, one of the finest men I have ever met. Every day when he gets up his first thought is that he must do his best to keep his company healthy. Why? Because he is intensely aware that many thousands of people depend on that for their jobs, and he feels he can't let them down. It is his duty as a Christian to make that company function to its utmost. It's not so that he'll make more money, either: he has more money than he will ever need, and he's given huge sums of it away. But he feels that God has given him a lot to be responsible for, and his duty is to take that responsibility with great seriousness. Other people's lives depend on him.

This is a responsibility all of us have, in some way. All of us have been given some area of responsibility—some people, some money, some things—that we have charge of. We can use them in the way a Christian ought to, or we can forget about relating them to God and go our own way, driven by impulses or greed. Those to whom God has given a lot have a special responsibility—nearly an awesome responsibility. I believe that this is what Jesus referred to when he said, "It is easier for a camel to go through the eye of a needle than for a rich man to enter the Kingdom of God." I think he was talking about a real camel and a real needle, the kind you sew with. What Jesus is saying is this: it may well be that your lifestyle can demonstrate where your heart really is. If seven-tenths of the world is starving, and you are rich, how you deal with that situation may indicate how you're dealing with Christ himself. Do you really love him more than your money? You say you do—but do you put your money on the line? James 2:14–26 develops this same idea when it says faith without works is dead. James doesn't mean that unless you act right God won't love you. He means that the overall pattern of your life may tell a lot about what your real relationship with the Lord is.

Sitting on top of all our material things, secure

financially, it's easy to talk about God. It may be that the discrepancy between the rich and poor is a test, a test to see if we really understand what spiritual life is all about, and are willing to follow it.

In fact, I've often wondered why God allows these four things on this earth: natural calamities like earthquakes or floods, sickness, the problem of race and the problem of poverty. What's so important about these, that he couldn't have designed the world a little differently?

One reason may be that these are the final exams for life. Take race as an obvious example. God could have made us all purple. Instead, he made us with various shades of color. Why? It's a test to see whether we really understand that love is not stopped by personal differences. Real Christian love isn't concerned with the color of someone's skin. If you say you love God but consistently hate your brother of another color, you're wrong in what you say about loving God. Your attitude toward others has shown it. The same is true if you say you love God, yet that love never seems to stir up any real compassion toward the poor, never really hurts your pocketbook. Your actions speak louder than your words.

the final word

We live in the richest country in the history of the world. Despite all economic problems we undergo, that remains true. And the Bible says, "From the person to whom much has been given, much will be required." We have been given a great deal—and with it goes a great responsibility. I wish there were hard-and-fast answers to the problems of that responsibility, rules like "Join the poverty ranks," or "Give a straight ten-percent tithe, no more, no less." But those answers aren't enough. I believe this is a problem every individual must struggle with, discussing it openly with his Christian friends and with God, studying the Bible and letting it determine the way he acts. The answers we find are going to be different ones—I know that in advance. The crucial questions to me are, "Are we wrestling with the problems at all? And are we acting?" For the way we handle our possessions has always been one of God's concerns. And for those of us who are rich in a world of poverty, his concern must be very great.

If you're in high school or college, you may doubt this applies to you. But it does. You have responsibility for a lot—not so much as your parents perhaps, but far more than a kid in India. What will you do with it? You are on the training grounds for life.

who's
prejudiced anymore?

**Whenever you look at someone and jump to conclusions—
that's prejudice. We're all affected.**

My father was not a Christian when I was growing up, but I learned more from him about God than some kids do from Christian fathers. I never heard him use a racially loaded sentence. He wouldn't permit certain words in our home—"kike," "nigger," "wop," "dago," "honky," "polock," "spic" and any words like them were out of bounds. He called people by their names, always.

From him I learned to loathe prejudice of any kind. It turns my stomach when I see people proud of the fact that they're inside while others are outside.

In this country the word "prejudice" brings to mind white attitude toward blacks, and rightly so. That's been the focal point of prejudice in this country for several hundred years, and we're still facing the awful consequences.

But if "prejudice" merely summons to mind movie stereotypes of Southern sheriffs in Alabama, or rock-throwing crowds in South Boston, then I doubt talking about it here will do much good. Is prejudice only something other people do? Let's broaden the definition a little. Prejudice is the uncomfortable feeling you get when somone strange tries to become a part of your lunch group. Prejudice is someone saying, "The teachers in this school really stink." Prejudice is feeling more afraid when you walk by a black person late at night than when you walk by a white person. Prejudice is joking about a fat person. Prejudice, for that matter, is thinking of a white Southern sheriff when I mention prejudice, rather than thinking of yourself. Prejudice is jumping to negative conclusions about any person without giving him a chance.

Prejudice comes out in a lot of subtle ways. Laughing at ethnic jokes is one way. Some people say, "Look, I know lots of Polish people, and they tell more Polock jokes than anyone." And that may be true. But they tell those jokes as a way of getting along with prejudiced people. They're kowtowing to the established ethnic stereotype, just as blacks in some areas are still sugary-sweet when they talk to whites, because they've learned that's what whites want.

Even the words we use can emphasize prejudice. I've heard people say, as a compliment, "That was white of him." That makes me feel sick. The bad guys in the movies always used to wear black; I think there was a subtle prejudice coming out of that which said, "Black is dirty, black is bad." Words and costumes are subtle, but they help build a powerful stereotype in our minds.

cringing inside

When I first went to college I thought I was thoroughly free from prejudice, probably because my family had always encouraged me to be. The first semester at college they had to put quite a few of us in what amounted to a barracks. One black guy already had a room, though, but no roommate. No one wanted to room with a black guy.

Partly because I wanted a room, and partly because I saw it as a chance to appear noble, I jumped at the chance. I learned a lot from the experience.

We got along very well, and there were always a bunch of black guys hanging around the room. I learned to understand black talk, to appreciate black music (When we were first rooming together, I came in and said, in all innocence, "What on earth is all that racket on the radio?" He said, "That's my home church."), and to enjoy being around him and his friends. But I do remember with shame, one particular moment. He was eating a popsicle and offered to split it with me. I took it, and I doubt anything showed on my face as I did, but I remember feeling an irrational sense of revulsion at eating something he had eaten from. When I realized what I was feeling, it shook me badly. I put the feeling in its place, and went ahead, but I don't think I ever again felt as though I were free from prejudice.

It was a small incident, but I never forgot it. These days, I get very suspicious when I hear people say, "Nobody is prejudiced here anymore," or "I don't see color. I love everyone exactly equally." Prejudice, whether over black and white, rich and poor, old and young, socially adept and klutzy, goes deep in our lives and I doubt it'll ever be eradicated short of heaven. It can be put in its place, and minimized, but let's quit kidding ourselves that we aren't prejudiced. Let's admit that we are, all of us. If you're less prejudiced than the guy down the block, or the guy in another part of the country, good. But don't pretend you're flawless.

Why is prejudice so deep-seated? It isn't something that just happens in America, you know. Virtually every country in the world has a problem with prejudice. In South Africa the whites dominate the blacks. In other parts of Africa one tribal group will dominate another. In France the French dominate the Arab immigrants. In India, under the caste system, the Brahmans have dominated the untouchables. In Israel the Jews dominate the Arabs. You can virtually make a rule: wherever there are two groups who are visibly different, there will be discrimination. The only exception would be when one group is so small its members are just a curiosity.

i'm afraid

Prejudice is universal because it plays on an emotion that's universal—fear. I see three kinds of fear operating.

First there's fear of losing your own self-esteem. Everyone wants to be important, but how do you measure whether you're important or not? Usually by comparing yourself with other people. Prejudice makes sure at least some people stay below your level. If your prejudice is powerful enough, and you happen to be a member of the group that's on top, you can **keep** the other people from achieving anything. Beyond that, by judging them without giving them a chance, you can dismiss what achievements they do make. You've already made up your mind, so facts don't matter. They can be rationalized. As far as you're concerned, you're superior.

Another aspect of fear has to do with money. In a free-market economy, there is competition for jobs, for a good education, for nice, quiet neighborhoods. So prejudice may come from the fear of losing the things you need—a job, a nice place to live, an education. It's easy for a well-to-do person to have a benign attitude—he's still got his income and his kids are still going to a nice school. I respect it more when a person from a lower-class background seems free from prejudice—it costs him something.

Finally there's the fear of differences. We like what we're used to, and when something comes in to disturb us it's easier to ridicule it than to understand it. This is particularly true of older people, because we have a stake in things staying the same. We want to stay comfortable and secure. We're afraid of change; we might lose everything we've worked for.

Of course, prejudice can be extended beyond these kinds of fear. There are leaders, often politicians, who manipulate people for their own ends. Fearful people band together for mutual defense. They make an attractive group for a leader who's looking for followers. Those leaders can manipulate the fear until prejudice becomes monstrous.

freedom now

I know of one high school in California that has three separate student governments: one Chicano, one black, one white. They have a race riot about once a year. There's an unwritten rule that each race uses its own rest room—go in the wrong one and you might be in trouble.

That's extreme, but then prejudice tends to go to extremes. Ten years ago people thought that, as soon as the problem was recognized, it would go away. It hasn't. It seems worse today, not better.

Prejudice has never created anything positive. All it's done is destroy people. It's destroying people in your school, in your city, right now. But very few people—not the kids in the California school, or their parents, or the administration—seem to have any idea what will set us free from it.

Jesus said, "You shall know the truth, and the truth shall set you free." That phrase has been inscribed over the gates of countless universities, and it's been used to support educational experiences as the key to true freedom. Generally people who use it ignore the fact that Jesus went on to say, "I am the Truth." But even accepting "truth" with a small "t" as the way to be set free makes a lot of sense.

So let's talk about the truth that will set you free from prejudice.

First there's the truth that all men are made in God's image, as equal beings that God loves equally. How can you fail to love someone when God made him? How can you consider him inferior when God doesn't?

Then there's the truth that all people are very much alike. You see differences at first, but when you begin to understand people you find they care about similar things—they just have different ways of expressing it. A farmer from a small town in Kansas whose car breaks down on the south side of Chicago is probably going to be scared to death—he's sure that everyone in that community is looking to rob him. But if that farmer moved to an integrated community there, if he worked and met people there, he'd be less afraid. He'd find all kinds of people there, many willing to help others, concerned about their family and friends. He'd know more of the truth, and be less afraid.

The more we come into contact with people unlike ourselves, the more we can understand them. School can play a great role in this by constantly exposing us to different ideas, different people.

That's the idea behind integrated schools. If we put the different races together, the reasoning goes, they'll learn more about each other and prejudice will be eliminated.

No doubt that **can** happen. But the record of the last ten years doesn't point overwhelmingly in that direction. Go into your average integrated high school and you won't discover that everything has become sweetness and light between the races. In many schools tension is worse. Putting the races in close physical proximity creates an opportunity for prejudice to wane, but it obviously doesn't guarantee it. Things can become worse, as they did in that California school.

white backlash

I have a good friend I thought was open-minded and not prejudiced—until he moved into a black community and had some bad experiences that reinforced the stereotype he'd heard about. Eventually he came to the conclusion blacks do not keep up their houses so well as whites . . . he said they smell . . . he decided they were lazy.

I sense a definite white, suburban, liberal back-lash against blacks right now, and it goes something like this: "We gave them every chance in the world to be nice white kids. They still talk like black kids, they act like black kids." As long as black people acted exactly as whites thought they should act, whites could overlook (maybe) their skin color. But whites are having a hard time dealing with a group of people who act and talk differently.

From this we learn that truth doesn't necessarily come with proximity. You don't necessarily under-stand someone just because you're in contact with him. Especially when there are really significant cultural differences, as there are between blacks and whites, it takes effort to break those barriers and understand people.

Take my friend, who became more prejudiced after coming into deeper contact with blacks. He decided blacks didn't keep up their houses so well as whites. But he didn't ask why they didn't in that particular situation. It could be the fact that they never could afford to own, but only to rent, had something to do with it. It could be a landlord over-charged and did nothing to help keep the place repaired. It could have had something to do with eight people living in a three-room house, or with the fact that the mother didn't have all day to do housework but had to work cleaning a white lady's house all day and came home exhausted, and no one else wanted to do the housework.

And it's possible that, at the bottom of it, there were some different values. It's possible some of those people didn't particularly like the style of life that is so neat it never has fun, that can't eat food in the living room, can't put feet on the furniture and spends all available time picking up. Whites have been saying for centuries that cleanliness is next to godliness, and we've got our values so confused we half-believe it. Actually, whether you want to live neat or cluttered is a choice that doesn't have morality on either side. And there are advantages either way.

And my friend discovered blacks smell. Well, so do whites, so do Europeans. I've heard Orientals complain about the way whites smell. Every race seems to have a distinctive odor. And of course, smell may have something to do with sharing a single shower with eight other people in a tenement.

Beyond that, the way people smell is very much dependent on how they were brought up. Europeans smell, and they don't change their clothes so often as Americans do, and they take a bath perhaps once a week. If you moved to Europe you'd have to learn to cope with that, and understand it. But because you don't have negative stereotypes about Europeans, it probably wouldn't be such an adjustment.

And in ancient cultures, people bathed perhaps once a year. Did you ever consider how the people in the Bible might have smlled?

Equal does not mean identical. Perhaps it would be nice if everyone in this country, or everyone in the world, were identical—if everyone thought the same, looked the same, talked the same, acted the same. They don't, however, and it may be a great thing that they don't, because it gives us some experience in learning to appreciate the variety that God apparently also appreciates, since he made things pretty varied. Blacks are not white. Indians are not blacks. Chicanos and Puerto Ricans are not identical. Chinese and Japanese have their own distinct values. They're equal not because they act and talk like whites if given the chance, but because God created them equal.

final solution

Truth in the form of education and exposure will free us from prejudice, but only to a point. If a black kid is sneered at by a white kid, he may realize that it's a product of the white kid's unbringing, but that bit of truth may not help alleviate prejudice against whites. If a blue-collar worker loses his job because his boss wants to hire one of his friend's sons, the worker may realize that this is just the way his boss affirms the value of friendship, but he'll still feel bitter about rich people. If a member of the Ku Klux Klan is so bedraggled and hopeless that the only way he can get self-esteem is by considering blacks inferior, integrating his kid's schools probably won't solve his problem. There is something greater than truth, and that is Truth. Jesus said, "I am the Way, the Truth, and the Life." The only real cure for prejudice, the only final cure, is continuous contact with him.

Why is that? Essentially because, when we encounter Christ, we are made aware of how completely undeserving of love we are—how thoroughly different we are from him. If anyone has a right to prejudice, it's God.

But he is not prejudiced. His love for us is total, completely accepting, always forgiving and understanding. God is so totally loving toward us that he defines the concept—God is love.

Someone really in touch with God is going to overflow with gratefulness. If you're not grateful, you don't understand what's happened. And when you're grateful to someone, you want to emulate him. If God hasn't discriminated against us, when he's had every right, how can we discriminate against others, when we have **no** right? Gratefulness is more than an intellectual realization—it goes into your emotions and personality. How can you help loving others when you're grateful for being loved yourself?

And this extends in all directions. Will Campbell is a Christian who was heavily involved in the first school integration in Little Rock, Arkansas. He held the hand of the first little black girl as she walked past the mobs of cursing, spitting whites. He had heard Jesus' statement, "Insofar as you do it to the least of my brethren, you did it to me." He thought that the little black girl qualified in that situation.

But years later he realized that the statement went in another direction, too. He began to work with the Grand Dragon of the Ku Klux Klan, trying to understand where his hurts were, and trying to minister to him. In some ways that Grand Dragon was the least of all God's children, for he had so little dignity himself he had to hate others.

Only a person who is really loved is free to love others. This is true in a family: those who come from a truly loving family know how to extend themselves to others. And this is true to a much greater extent of relating to God.

Now it has to be said, sadly, that Christians are not free from prejudice. In fact, it is to our shame that churches are full of prejudiced and racist people. It is to our shame that for years some churches taught that the Bible said blacks were inferior—which is absolutely a lie, without a shred of evidence. I don't think Christians had better go around claiming to be the perfect people. I do think that when we truly realize what God has done, we see how evil our own prejudice is. I believe we can honestly claim to people that the love of God is the only final antidote to prejudice—ours or theirs. If we want to be free from prejudice, we need to come into closer and deeper contact with him.

bloody noses

Philosophizing is fine. But what about those who come home with bloody noses? If you go to a troubled racially-mixed school, it's possible you'll be beaten up once or twice. If you own property in an area that is rapidly changing racially, you may lose money because of the real-estate devaluations. Even if you befriend a stranger, your old gang might drop you. There are many situations where we are suffering because of the sins of the generations before us; for instance, the racism of whites toward blacks for hundreds of years is coming out in the attitudes some blacks hold toward whites. Or the fact that your grandfather stole Indian land may make it difficult for an Indian to trust you. Unfair it is, but you can't wipe out history in a day.

The book of 1 Peter has some wonderful advice for this kind of situation. It may be hard to stomach at first, but think about it. "A man does a fine thing when he endures pain . . . though he knows he is suffering injustly. After all, it is no credit to you if you are patient in bearing a punishment which you have richly deserved! But if you do your duty and are punished for it and can still accept it patiently, you are doing something worthwhile in God's sight. Indeed, this is your calling. For Christ suffered for you and left you a personal example, so that you might follow in his footsteps. He was guilty of no sin nor of the slightest prevarication. Yet when he was insulted he offered no insult in return" (1 Pet. 2:19–23, Phillips).

Peter is writing to people who understand suffering. They are living in a cruel society, the Roman empire. They're Christians, and some of their fellow-Christians are dying. All of them can tell stories about friends who've been hassled or beat up.

How does his advice apply to a racial situation today? Well, suppose you are in a school where racial tension is high. People get beat up; you're afraid. You realize, perhaps, that people are acting this way because of the past injustices and sins, yet at the same time you can't excuse individuals for their cruelty and prejudice.

The point Peter makes is, in a tense situation

some people are going to be hurt. You can't help that. But there are two possible ways to suffer.

The first is to get involved in the problem. You can say, "Nobody can treat me like that. Those people are animals, and I have a right to defend myself. If they're that kind of people, I'll treat them like they deserve." And in that case, you'll become part of the problem, and you'll suffer for it.

The other choice is to do no wrong, and suffer unjustly. You can love people in your school, you can talk to them and try to help them understand each other, and yet if tensions are bad you'll get hurt at times. Evil doesn't disappear overnight. But, Peter suggests, it's much better to suffer when you've done nothing to make the situation worse, because that's exactly the way Jesus suffered.

In a prejudiced society, someone is going to get hurt. Let's make sure Christians get hurt for doing what's loving and right, not for being as hate-filled as other people.

Pain is not the worst thing that can happen to you. We usually think it is, so we run away. We avoid potentially painful situations. We withdraw into our own little safe, prejudiced groups. But pain makes you grow. It makes you face yourself, and examine yourself. It stretches you.

God's final exam

Why did God make us all different? He didn't have to. Maybe part of it was a kind of final exam. Through him we learn that he loves us all, even though we're different from him and don't deserve to be loved. We learn that he loves all of us equally, that we're all his children. We learn that Jesus loved us enough to come and take risks, and get involved with people who weren't like him in some very important respects, and that he loved those people right to the day they killed him.

We know all that. But do we really? Is it just words, or do you really feel it? The differences God has made give us an authentic test. If you say you understand, but you're still prejudiced, you've failed the test and need some remedial work.

And that goes for all differences, not just racial ones. There are kids in your neighborhood who don't get along with others like most people do; they're misfits. There are older people. There are people who look funny. How do you handle them? How do you treat strangers? How do you treat people in competition with you for something you really want? Do you love them, or do you exclude them? If you don't love them, you haven't fully internalized what God has done for you.

why believe in Jesus?

"So your thing is religion. Great.
But why should I believe it?

Why do I believe Christianity is true? Let me tell you a story.

Once upon a time, someone parachuted a wrist watch into a remote tribal village in Sumatra. They did it at night, so the villagers, who had never contacted civilization, only heard a tremendous, frightening roar pass over. The next morning someone peeked out of his hut to find the watch lying there.

None of them had seen anything like it; they gathered around jabbering and pointing, calling others to see the curious object.

After minutes of poking and looking, someone got the courage to pick it up. He smiled—it was smooth and cool to the touch, more so than any stone polished by a stream. He held it to his ear and let out an amazed yell—it ticked! Others grabbed it from his hand so they could listen as well.

Of course, people had work to do, and not everyone sat around looking at the watch. But there were some whose work was so well organized they had the free time to sit and pass it back and forth, studying its properties. There was a lot to study.

The watch stayed in the tribe for many years, and gradually many pieces of information were discovered about it. Fairly early, someone noticed that one of the hands went around in a circle. A little later someone realized that every time that hand went around once, another hand moved one click! that led to an even more astonishing discovery (which took years)—when that hand clicked all the way around once, the smallest hand moved from one marking to the next. When that smallest hand had passed all the markings twice, the sun came up!

Evidently, the sun and the watch worked together. Perhaps it was the watch that made the sun come up! Could it be their tribe had found the regulator of the universe? That theory was strengthened when someone discovered that the moon, in a very complicated way, was also linked to the watch.

People were a bit afraid of the watch. They remembered the terrifying roar that had accompanied its coming, and lots of theories were developed to explain its origin. Some said a giant wasp had dropped it. Others suggested it came from a flying lion, roaring through the heavens. Out of fear, some wanted to put the watch in a special strongbox, where only the witch doctor would look at it. They were afraid of it because they thought it controlled the sun and moon, and the idea of a giant wasp or flying lion was not very comforting.

Another group was less afraid, more interested in studying it. They realized that by studying it, they could discover something about the maker; they weren't sold on the flying lion theory. And they noticed many things. First of all, the watch was symmetrical and predictable, not random. Secondly, it was durable—the maker must have had a concern for durability and function. Third, it was beautiful—it shone more than anything they had seen. The maker must love beauty. They concluded that the roaring lion theory, at least as it had been put forward, was wrong. Lions aren't too concerned with beauty or with order. But having given up the roaring lion theory, these village scientists developed a powerful curiosity about what **had** made it. He must be very powerful. He must have a powerful understanding of the totality of the universe, to link a small shiny object to the sun and moon. And he must be interested in order and beauty.

The really interesting fact, however, is that no one in the whole village ever suggested that no one had made the watch—that it had just happened.

a world like a watch

If you look at our world, you'll find some strong similarities to the watch. First, it's orderly. There is some controversy in physics whether at the basic level things behave randomly or not, but at the level of astronomy there's no real argument. You can tell what time the sun will come up fifty years from today—it's very predictable.

And the earth is durable. It can be damaged, of course, but it doesn't occasionally go zinging toward the sun, or threaten to suddenly crumble. We've been here for thousands of years and only discovered ecology a few years ago—the earth must be fairly durable to endure thousands of years of mining it, digging canals and setting off bombs and building fires and killing animals. And obviously, the world is beautiful—far more beautiful than anything the greatest artist has ever done.

Down through history, most men have concluded that, like the watch, the world must have a maker. They differed as to what he was like—some theories were similar to the roaring lion theory—but most men, until the last one hundred years, believed that there was someone behind the earth we live in—a creator.

Recently, however, there are some suggesting

where the villagers never imagined—that there is no maker, that the world just happened. The argument is, if you don't mind my simplifying, like this: we understand how the world works in the minutest detail. We can explain and even duplicate many things that baffled our forefathers. Therefore, there is no God. Belief in him is outmoded; we don't need him to explain things.

That argument sounds suspiciously like this one: My father built a house. I studied the house, and learned how it is made. I can now build a house. Therefore my father did not exist.

I'm just making the point that most men, confronted with a something similar to our earth, would assume a maker was responsible. Nothing I understand in modern science makes that a less likely proposition.

If you read Romans 1, you find this basic thought: that everyone can know there is a God by looking at the world. Not only that, though; Paul claims you can know something about the character of God. In other words, he says the universe itself is grounds for knowing that the maker is not fierce and amoral like a roaring lion or giant wasp. But why does he say that?

right and wrong

Part of his reasoning must be based on the order, durability and beauty of the world. I think it goes beyond that, however. We can say we know the Creator cares about whether we do right or wrong.

Why? Because included in what the Creator made are human beings. They always care about right and wrong. Their societies always have rules. Some of those rules are simply good sense for preservation, but some are constructed to protect the weak from the strong. There are very few societies where it is considered good to betray a friend. Sooner or later, when people argue politics or law, you hear someone say something like "We ought not to do that." But why not? Simply because there is something built into us that holds to right and wrong.

Right and wrong aren't just a frill, either; they're very basic. If you're in the hands of torturers who think nothing of killing you or making you suffer inconceivably, you have only one power. But it is a very great power. Deep in your soul you can say, "I am right. I am on the side of truth."

Solzhenitsyn, in writing of the terror of brutal torture in Soviet prison camps, wrote this:

> So what is the answer? How can you stand your ground when you are weak and sensitive to pain, when people you love are still alive, when you are unprepared?
>
> What do you need to make you stronger than the interrogator and the whole trap?
>
> From the moment you go to prison you must put your cozy past firmly behind you. At the very threshold, you must say to yourself: "My life is over, a little early to be sure, but there's nothing to be done about it. I shall never return to freedom. I am condemned to die— now or a little later. But later on, in truth, it will be even harder, and so the sooner the better. I no longer have any property whatsover. For me those I love have

died, and for them I have died. From today on, my body is useless and alien to me. Only my spirit and my conscience remain precious and important to me."

Confronted by such a prisoner, the interrogation will tremble.

Only the man who has renounced everything can win that victory.*

There is tremendous power in the man who holds on to his conscience when everything else is gone. Why? Because every man—even his torturer—knows inside that something is right and something wrong. It seems a fair assumption that whoever or whatever made him holds that same standard. We call that maker "God."

christians say more

This is a basic idea of Christianity. However, it is also the basic idea behind most other religions. When people say, "All religions teach the same thing," they couldn't be much more wrong. The different religions have vastly different ways of looking at the world. But in this respect they are largely in agreement: there is a God who controls the world, and we ought to please him.

But how to please him? Most religions suggest that by learning truth and obeying rules, by meditating or attending worship, man raises himself to a place where he can contact God. Christians hold that this is impossible. God is so high that raising

---

*Alexander Solzhenitsyn, **The Gulag Archipelago, 1918–1956: An Experiment in Literary Investigation,** (New York: Harper and Row, 1974), p. 130.

yourself to reach him is like standing on someone's shoulders to touch the moon. Instead, Christians claim that God has come down to us.

Any "proof" of Christianity must go back to Jesus Christ himself. He did exist in history; he is not a mythical figure. We have original historical documents written by eyewitnesses. It is amazing to me how many people who argue against Christianity have never even read those documents. They argue on the basis of a misty memory of Sunday School combined with something they heard in a history class. The source documents are easy to get, but they've never bothered! It's as though someone were arguing that Shakespeare's plays were nothing especially good, and you discovered during the argument that he'd never read any of them.

Just on the basis of intellectual honestly we can encourage people to read the New Testament and find out the facts. We can encourage them to confront Jesus Christ and what he really was like. After all, Christianity stands or falls on the basis of whether Jesus was really God; shouldn't we all get away from our images of him and discover whether he really measures up to what's claimed? When you read the New Testament, you don't get ideas of Jesus as simply a wise teacher or the 'original pacifist. What strikes you first of all is his audacity; he isn't the head of anything, and he goes around trailed by the dregs of humanity, yet he talks as though he's king! He doesn't care what people think of him, yet he's not arrogant; he's humble enough to care about the smallest, saddest person in the crowd. The truth he speaks is irrefutable; the wisest men are left sputtering. Yet he talks about his "kingdom" and even when they take him to the real king, who can have him killed by flicking his finger, Jesus acts more as though the tables were reversed and the king was **his** subject. Even death, according to the New Testament, could not rule over him; he won the battle with it and came back to life.

Read the New Testament, and see if Jesus is a person you can conveniently label "great teacher." If he was a great teacher and nothing more, why does he talk the way he does? The best teacher in your school would soon be carted away if he started talking about his "kingdom," intimating that he had a special, unique relationship to God, that in fact he and God the Father "are one," and saying he was the only road to God. As C. S. Lewis pointed out, Jesus was either a fraud, as crazy as a man who thinks he's a poached egg, or he was what he said he was.

Of course, some suggest that the writers of the New Testament hedged on the truth quite a bit in order to make a religion out of it. A lot of people have spent time trying to separate the real Jesus from what was added later on. The idea that Jesus rose again from the dead has been a chief target.

But what happened to those men? In every case we know of, history records that the disciples died for what they believed. Remember, Christianity was not the popular thing when it started. You could be killed for believing it, and many were. Men don't usually die defending something they know is a lie —especially when the very cause they're dying for places a high premium on telling the truth. If you're going to die for something, you want to get the facts straight.

sky-writing proof?

I've given you some of the best reasons I know for believing Christianity. There are plenty of other ways to argue for the same thing: by looking at how Bible prophecies came true, or how archeology validates the Bible. If you're looking for proof, however—proof as tangible and obvious as skywriting —you won't find it. The arguments that Christianity is true are strong ones; I've sketched them here, and if you're interested in more depth you should read something like C. S. Lewis' **Mere Christianity.** But intelligent, honest men disbelieve. Sometimes you might hear a Christian speaker talk about evidence in favor of Christianity with such power you're absolutely sure there's no debating it. You leave saying inside, "Gotcha!" However, I can assure you there are intelligent people who build a powerful case in the opposite direction. It depends a lot on who holds the microphone.

Are we caught in the middle, tempted to throw all arguments, pro and con, away? Should we stop using our minds and "just believe?" No. We ought to use our minds to their utmost, and then "just believe."

For there is a point beyond which your mind cannot take you. After you've gone through all the intellectual questions about Christianity, there is still a choice to be made. It is a choice of faith. It is a decision about who you will ultimately trust, and about what kind of life you believe in your heart is right.

What is it that lets me put my faith in God? It's not simply intellectual arguments. It's the realization that Jesus is the central piece of the puzzle of my life—that he makes sense of things.

I can remember speaking at a college once, and afterwards walking home with one of the professors. He didn't believe in Christ, but he seemed to be honestly searching. He had many, many questions. There wasn't time to answer them all, and when we parted he said, with deep feeling, "Pray for me, Jay. I want to believe, but I can't."

the impossible dream

Non-Christians aren't always people in angry, sarcastic, argumentative rebellion against God. I find many like that professor, wanting to believe but not seeing that it is possible. For them, it's important first to show that Christianity is believable—that there is a good basis for accepting what Christ said as genuine. And perhaps they have special questions that need to be answered; this professor was a scientist and needed to be shown (probably by other scientists, through books) that there was no necessary contradiction between science and Christianity.

But those answers are not enough. The scientist would have to see that there was more to life than science. There are mysteries beyond the atom. Every relationship, for example, is a deep mystery.

There is no pill or treatment for loneliness. There is no way to penetrate a person's life who will not let you love him or her. Sociology, psychology, physics or biology are useless when you are trying to help someone who will not be helped, or trying to change your own self so you'll stop hurting people. There is a deep reality of sin in human beings. There is also a deep appreciation of beauty, of truth, of love, that is not explained or helped apart from God.

When you come to Jesus Christ with all these things he makes sense. It's like working a picture puzzle: you can often get stuck on one central piece. Until you get that piece, nothing works. You may try to force the wrong piece in, or even whittle a little bit of it away to make it fit. But when you have the right piece, all the others begin to fall in place—not instantly, not easily—but they do fall in place.

The Bible says, "Taste and see that the Lord is good." There is this experimental side of finding the truth. There are many ways of looking at the world, but only one in which all the pieces really seem to fit. There may be many doubts, many pieces that are unfound, but there is also a sense that the searching is on the right track, for you have found the right central piece in Jesus Christ.

Elton Trueblood expressed this in **A Place to Stand.** Archimedes wrote that "if you give me lever and a place to stand, I can move the world." Trueblood uses that idea to say that Jesus Christ is a place to stand—a center from which the other pieces of your world can be moved.

So much of the Christian message seems, on experience, consistent with the way the world is. For example, Christianity has always said men are sinful; now, after years of the world's acting as though it wasn't so, the famous Karl Menninger writes a book called **Whatever Happened to Sin?** Christianity was right after all. The pieces seem to fit. There are other ways of looking at the world, but the pieces keep having to be moved and changed. They don't fit right.

Ultimately, if you're considering trusting Christ, you aren't confronted with ideas alone. You're confronted with God. It's a very personal decision— whom will you believe? Who will you trust? No one can ever prove to you conclusively that faith in God won't end up disappointing you. Certainly faith in God will never turn out to bring exactly the rewards you hoped, because we never manage to understand God completely. His thoughts are bigger than ours; his plans are bigger than ours.

Ultimately you must choose, not because some Christian argues you to the point of giving up, but because there is a person confronting you—Jesus Christ. He can't be ignored. You have to turn toward him, or else turn away. The arguments in his favor are powerful, but won't take you to true faith. In my own life, it was a question of trust—whom I would rely on. I chose Jesus.

what's so personal about God?

**God isn't content to communicate with the masses.
He wants to talk to you—alone!**

In college I once had the honor of being chairman of a religious emphasis week. The college brought in a special speaker, and he was introduced to the faculty in a special meeting. I was the only student there. It was an imposing situation, because, naturally, everyone there was older and far more educated than I. But somehow in the course of discussion I mentioned that I prayed and that I knew God heard me pray.

To give the faculty credit, they didn't just pass it off with an amused smile. They listened and questioned me. "How do you know God hears you? How do you know you're not just talking into the air?"

If I were asked that now I might say some things about the character of God—that he is not the kind of God who doesn't listen. But perhaps my answer then was just as effective. "Well, I just **know**. The Spirit bears witness with my spirit that I'm a child of God."

"Well," someone said, "you could be undergoing some sort of psychological experience, imagining a response from God that isn't objectively there at all."

I didn't know what to say. I remember looking desperately around the room at the faces of those alert, intelligent men and women I respected so much. I saw one of the profs I knew rather well. His wife was with him. "Doctor," I asked, "do you love your wife?"

"Yes," he said.

Then I turned to his wife. "Do you love your husband?" She said yes also.

I turned back to the prof. "How do you know she loves you?"

He said, "She tells me so."

I asked his wife, and she said the same thing.

I said, "You know, you could be lying to each other. You think everything's fine, but Doctor, your wife could be carrying on on the side. She might be **saying** all those things about love just to keep you from knowing the truth."

"No," he said, "when you love someone and you know them well, you know things are right."

"Well," I said, "it's the same thing between God and me. There's a communication that goes beyond words when you love someone."

I realize now that you can overstress that intimate aspect of relating to Christ. Still, it's basic; Christianity is not a dry collection of facts about God. Christians don't simply know **about** God, they know **him.** When the Bible talks about that personal involvement, it talks about the Holy Spirit.

There are many pitfalls in trying to define the Holy Spirit. People have killed each other arguing over definitions of the Trinity, of God the Father, the Son and the Holy Spirit. I don't intend to get involved in that. It's clear to me, though, that when we talk about the direct communication of God to man, we're talking about the Holy Spirit. The Spirit is a way in which God, not using a physical body, can exist in the world and communicate with his own people, yet not destroy their independence.

Before Jesus left our planet, he promised that he would send the Holy Spirit. In fact, he said it was

better for us if he left, because otherwise the Holy Spirit would not come. Now why was it better? A lot of people look back on the disciples and figure, "Man, if I'd been with them, it'd have been easy. I could have physically seen and touched Jesus. My faith would never waver."

But suppose Jesus were here, physically, today. He could only be one place at one time. Probably he'd stay in Jerusalem, and you'd have to save your money to take a once-in-a-lifetime excursion to see him. Once you arrived, you'd have to fight the crowds. Perhaps, if you were lucky, you'd get in to see him with a group of others. He might say a few words, shake hands with everyone and answer a couple questions. Naturally, there wouldn't be time for everyone's questions. Then the time would be up and you'd be ushered out, and the next group would come in to see him.

For the rest of your life you'd try to remember that moment. But your memory would fade, and you'd lose touch with him. Furthermore, you might not have a complete picture. If you saw him on a day similar to the day he chased the money changers out the temple your view would be different from "Let the little children come to me, for of such is the kingdom of God."

But because we have the Holy Spirit, we don't have these problems. The Spirit is Christ speaking to each of us at any time. He is not limited by geography. And because he speaks to us through the Bible, we get a balanced point of view. Our encounter with Jesus Christ isn't limited to a few moments; it takes in hundreds of the most important things he did and said in his life. I don't think there's anything in Christianity more exciting and joyful than the doctrine of the Holy Spirit. It means that I'm special to God. God is not content to give himself to the masses; he wants to give himself to me. He wants to know me. He wants to help **me** as I struggle my way through life.

grasshopper God

Unfortunately, we can't talk about the Holy Spirit without getting rid of some misconceptions. For many of us the Holy Spirit has become not a loving person, but a thing.

My worst experience of this came in a small community. I was speaking there for a week. After the first meeting one sane-appearing, middle-aged man came up and said, "You know, in this community you're going to find that things are a little different."

I said, "How's that?"

"Well, in this community the Holy Spirit is a jumper."

"A jumper?" I said.

"Well, yeah, he'll be at one church for a while, and then he'll jump over to another church. I've watched it over the years. He just jumps from church to church."

I hardly knew where to start with the guy. He apparently envisioned the Holy Spirit as a large grasshopper. Not that he was a jerk of any kind. He was just a local businessman who'd served in churches in the area, had watched and listened to what people said.

You won't find too many people talking about the Holy Spirit as a "jumper," but there are two tendencies that, combined, come up to something not too far off. They're both misconceptions of the Holy Spirit.

The first comes from trying to visualize the Holy Spirit. He's invisible, but the way most of our minds work, we don't totally accept that. Some of our ideas come from the movies. I remember in **The Ten Commandments** Cecil B. DeMille portrayed the Spirit of the Lord as a dark fog coming down the street, killing all the baby Egyptians. Some of us have a "fog" image of the Holy Spirit.

Or the Spirit is a little man about the size of a Jesus statue riding on someone's dash, and he "lives inside our hearts."

To a degree, these images are inevitable and harmless. But they are certainly not very warm, are they? They're not very personable, are they?

We need to come back, in all our thinking, to the fact that the Spirit is a person. He is, in fact, Jesus Christ, speaking to us individually and personally.

Since the Holy Spirit is a person, we expect to see him affecting people differently from a force or an object. Forces push you around; a person who loves you can affect your whole personality, but he does it subtly, lovingly. If you have a friend whom you admire, I'm sure that whether you realize it or not, you've changed through that friend. But the change is of a whole different type from what would be brought by, say, catching the measles. Yet sometimes we think of the Spirit as a kind of holy measles. He's not. He's a person.

The other misconception is more subtle, but it's dangerous too. We sing the song, "There's a sweet, sweet Spirit in this place, and I know it is the Spirit of the Lord." In a sense, that's right, because when Christians are gathered together to worship God and sing, the feelings they share **are** prompted by the presence of God. The danger is in thinking that there's no difference between a group spirit and the Holy Spirit.

You know, if you're feeling lousy, it doesn't mean the Spirit has left you. In fact, it's in that situation he most wants to comfort you.

If we think the Spirit is nothing more than a group spirit, we go around constantly looking for the group that's "on fire." But the Holy Spirit doesn't follow good feelings around like a dog on a leash. He's to be found wherever Christians are, not wherever good feelings are. You can create a certain atmosphere, or spirit, but that doesn't mean it has much depth or that the Spirit of God is particularly involved. Woodstock proved that.

The man who thought the Holy Spirit was a "jumper" evidently thought you could track the Holy Spirit by following the path of excitement. Probably everytime a church got excited, someone said, "You can really feel the Spirit." Well, the Holy Spirit is exciting at times. But he's also a "still, small voice" that isn't spectacular at all. He's also present when a single individual stands out against greed and oppression, and is laughed at for his pains.

your mind matters

If you wrote down everything the Bible says about the Holy Spirit, and took time to talk about each thing, you would have a long book. I'd rather talk about a few of the things that seem most important to our generation.

Let's start by talking about what business the Holy Spirit is in. We think, sometimes, that the Holy Spirit is a kind of tool we use to get things from God. If we treat him right, we think, we'll get what we want. Or we use him as a stamp of approval on what we believe, or on our good feelings. "The Spirit told me this, so I did it." But the Holy Spirit is really here to teach me about Christ. He always shows off Christ, never himself, and he is helping us understand and live the full, balanced truth about God and ourselves.

That's why Martin Luther and many others in the Reformation came up with a very important principle, which they called "Spirit and Word." They said, the Spirit never works where the Bible is not at work. And the Bible never works in people's lives unless the Spirit is there. If you find one, you're bound to find the other.

Now this doesn't mean that the Bible is a kind of fourth part of the Trinity. It just means that the Spirit consistently uses the Word. He wants to communicate to us, he wants to do it clearly and without stuttering, and he wants to speak so that everyone will be able to understand, not just a few. We believe God gave us the Bible to do those very things.

Therefore, the Spirit is never involved with turning off your mind. You can't turn off your mind, turn up your emotions and really understand the Bible. Yes, you can read the Bible like a comic strip, catching a verse here and a story there, and never putting it all together. Some do that. Some of these people even give up Christ and the Bible because all they can remember is David and Goliath, and they've forgotten the character of Jesus and the power of the things he said. But if someone claims he's got a message from the Spirit of God, he had better be able to put it in touch with what the whole Bible says. They will never contradict each other; they will support and validate each other.

The Holy Spirit offers us intimacy with God. We are his sons and daughters, and it is the Spirit who assures us of that. Nothing could be more strengthening and helpful than being able to call out to God as a father. But some people take the intimacy farther; they seem not only to believe that God speaks to them, but also that they can speak for God. They feel they've been specially singled out to speak or lead in a completely authoritative way.

Well, there's some indication in Scripture that this is possible. When the Old Testament prophets stood up to speak, they felt they were speaking for God. But there's also plenty of indication that they weren't the only ones claiming it. There were ten false spokesmen for every one who really was dealing with the truth. But the false ones, of course, never got their words written down in the Bible.

So when we're confronted with someone who's claiming to have a pipeline to God, I think we ought to check him out a little. The Bible calls this "testing the spirits."

I recently heard from a girl I've known for some time. She's been through some difficult experiences, and she's very emotionally unstable. She's got a problem with alcohol, and she's extremely distraught. Now she's met some young men who are filled with the Spirit and say they are shepherds. Each of them has a little group, eight or ten people, primarily young women, who work and turn their money over to the shepherd. They aren't supposed to do anything without first consulting the shepherd. All this because these young men feel this is something God asked them to do.

Now, really, this is hard to judge. This particular girl, and probably many of the others, really could use the guidance of a good substitute father. But is it a biblical pattern for one person to take over the mind of another adult and control her? I would say no.

I think there are several questions you have to ask about what you hear. First, does it fit with the biblical pattern? Then, does it go against natural law? We're not encouraged to go against gravity by jumping off buildings, no matter how "spiritual" it seems. Is it in line with the experience of other Christians? Do other wise and experienced Christians agree that it is the will of God? All these questions should be asked, and particularly asked of an individual who has set himself above everyone else. On the whole, the Spirit is very democratic. He speaks to everyone who knows God, not just through certain highly spiritual people. So someone who sets himself or herself up as having a special message should be carefully examined.

gifted people

To speak of the Holy Spirit and not talk about the gifts of the Spirit would be a terrific oversight. There is plenty of controversy about the gifts these days, and of course the Bible places fairly heavy emphasis on them.

It's amazing how blind we can be. If you read the parts of the Bible that talk about the gifts—Romans 12, 1 Corinthians 12, Ephesians 4—you get a very clear general picture. It goes like this: God gives every Christian a special ability or set of abilities that can't be explained simply by training or natural talent. Every Christian is **different,** and has a unique contribution to make to other Christians. Every Christian's gifts are essential; you can't say any person is unnecessary. God has given each of us a wonderful role to play.

So why is it so often true that when people talk about the gifts, they end up talking as though everybody ought to be the same? If the message of the gifts of the Spirit is that every Christian is important and necessary, why do we end up feeling inadequate, as though someone else got a better deal?

If you go to a wedding and the mother of the bride cries while the groom's mother laughs, do you assume that one loves her child and the other doesn't? No, of course you realize that God has given them different personalities and they respond to the same event in different ways. And why do you think we have four accounts in the Bible of one man's life? Each gospel shows a different reaction to one man. This is the chief lesson of the gifts. One man's view is not enough to get a total picture of Jesus. We needed four. One way of responding to the Holy Spirit is not enough. We need many. One kind of ability and giftedness is not enough for a group of Christians. We need all kinds.

I don't think we necessarily need to look at the lists of gifts mentioned in the Bible and get terrifically detailed about who has which ones. I don't think those lists are meant to be exhaustive. Too often we see the trees and miss the forest. The overall point is that, in the work the Spirit does in our lives, everyone is essential, and everyone is different. We should quit trying to cram each other into molds. The Spirit never does.

less than human

Sometimes you hear people talk about being "led by the Spirit." At times they will go even farther and speak of being "Spirit-controlled." That raises another observation I'd like to make on the Holy Spirit. Someone has said it this way: "The Holy Spirit is a gentleman. He will never come into a situation unless you ask him to."

This is in opposition to what some people seem to mean when they talk about being controlled by the Spirit. They seem to have the heavenly side of Flip Wilson's "the devil made me do it" in mind.

There is a powerful temptation to become less

than human, to turn off our minds and let feelings push us around, or to let someone else tell us what to do. I don't believe this is ever the work of the Holy Spirit. The emotions are to have full play, but so is the mind. You see, God loves **you**—not your carcass. If he needed a body to push around, he could make another one very quickly. He wants you to develop into the full person you were made to be.

The Spirit is involved in many other areas of our lives—in fact, in every area. He's the interpreter of our prayers; I'm sure that many things we ask for are absolutely impossible, not because they're scientifically impossible, but because they violate the whole scheme God is developing. But the Spirit goes beyond our words and understands what we really want.

It is the Holy Spirit who produces love, joy, peace, patience and the other Christian virtues in our lives.

It is the Holy Spirit who continually stands, through men's conscience, for a right way, so that there is never a lack of right to judge wrong by, and so that men are, at some level, conscious of their need for God's forgiveness.

It is the Holy Spirit who impregnates our minds with God's wisdom, so that we can make the right decisions when we have to choose. He even overrules our judgement and points us in another direction when we're off the track.

I could go on and on. There's no limit to what the Holy Spirit does, because there is no limit to the involvement God wants to have in your life. He involves himself with you through the Holy Spirit.

who's got the spirit?

Christians seem to be having some trouble with the Holy Spirit lately, fighting over who has him, who's **really** listening to him, and what you have to do to get him.

I don't think the fighting is at all necessary, except perhaps in some extreme cases. There are three general ways we are involved with God's Spirit, and I think the problem lies in emphasizing one over the others.

First, we receive God's Spirit when we become Christians. There can't be any argument over that; read Romans 8:9. You don't receive a chunk of him with more to come; you can't divide a person into pieces. You receive all of him.

But since it's a beginning relationship, you don't know all there is to know about him. In fact, you probably don't know much at all. So it's natural that, as time goes by, you learn more about him, and more about yourself. That's the second thing the Spirit does—teach you and help you grow. It may be that your growth will be gradual, and it may come in big quantum jumps. If you go through a tremendous jump, you'll be tempted to look back and say, "I didn't know anything before." And you'll be tempted to look around at everyone else whose experience is different, and consider them lacking something.

But that would be a terrible mistake. God, remember, is not speaking to the masses through his Spirit; he is speaking to individuals. Each person has his own way of growth, and you can only superficially compare it to others.

The final thing the Spirit does in our lives is perfect us. None of us has seen that yet; we will see that when we see Christ face-to-face, and become like him. It's important to remember that this is still to come, because sometimes we get the impression that we've arrived. No way. We may know more of God than we did a year ago, but compared to what there is to know, we know nothing.

We're on the road, and the Holy Spirit is leading us, helping us, comforting us and speaking to us. To him, each one of us is special, and he treats us as individuals.